# EVOLUTION
### OF
# HUMAN BEINGS
### AND
# SOCIETY

# EVOLUTION
## OF
# HUMAN BEINGS
## AND
# SOCIETY

LAXMI NAYARAN

PARTRIDGE

| ISBN: | Softcover | 978-1-4828-7017-6 |
| | eBook | 978-1-4828-7016-9 |

This book is an outpouring of a disillusioned heart on democratic anarchism by **20% burgeon People over 80% BPL & APL categories of people**.

Print information available on the last page.

**To order additional copies of this book, contact**
Partridge India
000 800 10062 62
orders.india@partridgepublishing.com

www.partridgepublishing.com/india

# CONTENTS

DEDICATED TO MY FATHER

# Acknowledgements

I am extremely grateful to **Shri Neepesh Chandra Talukdar**, IAS **(Retd.), retired Member of Posts and Telegraphs Board, New Delhi, India** for contributing a foreword, which lands distinction to my humble work. Also to **Mother, Mahasveta Devi**, eminent writer and recipient of **Jnanpith Award & Raman Megasaysay Award** for contributing a forward for wide circulation of this **Book** especially to the society of young generation. I would also like to thank the editors for their enthusiastic support throughout the preparation of this book.

# INTRODUCTION

This Book is a true story of a senior citizen, **(Sukumar Banerjee)** in short **"SB"** who unluckily has come back to Kolkata after 40 years to stay permanently in his original Parental House. His return, instead of bringing joys, has caused miseries, which are caused to systems and cultures so far developed in the society. He felt sorry to see the working systems in all Government departments influenced by political parties' dictatorship. The atmosphere is vitiated and is poisoning people like opium in the way of raising slogans, holding of processions, staging of strikes etc. which are destroying human relations mentally, physically, religiously and also economically, thereby preventing all constructive works designed for development of the state and country as a whole. His ambition is to fulfill his respected father's vision, construction of **BRIDHYASHRAM (Old-Age-Home)** for giving succour to senior citizens, those who are living in isolation left by their near and dear ones. Parents bring up their children with high hope and expectation that they would look after them in their old age and give them relief, in obedience to their duties and responsibilities and on humanitarian grounds. The situation has deteriorated so much so that the children do not even care to enquire about their parents' welfare. The social structure has become so nauseating that in families below poverty line, in the course of their wife's failure to get money from their parents' house, wife is not spared from physical torture. **SB** finds that the senior citizens are turning into a fast growing **APARTHIED** in the society. The situation, as described above highlights the urgent need of setting up some **Old-Age-Homes (BRIDHYASHRAMS)** in various parts of the country. It would be worthwhile to mention here that our Honourable Prime Minister has been gracious enough to announce that the Government would look after senior citizens of the country. Establishment of **BRIDHYASHRAMS (Old-Age- Homes)** will be a philanthropic step in this direction. But the democratic systems in our country run by liaise fare with the power of fundamental rights to boost up the growth of profits of Industrialists and business communities will make the laughing stock announcement of looking after the senior citizens by Prime Minister. Now the Government is thinking to amend the RTI Act to crash the peoples' voice against corruptions. Present central Government is trying to unite with the various numbers of States Governments administered by corrupted/criminal leaders of political parties.

**There was a message, from educationist and great orator, Bipin Chandra Pal, which is published by the Editor of 'Statesman' on 22 May 1932 that "Democracies are notoriously ungrateful. They use man to the utmost limit for their physical and mental power and discard them and throw them on the scrapheap". This message is true to the knowledge of every politically educated person who understood that the present so-called democracies have**

become weapons for some group of KING–PARTIES as dictator to rule this democratic country in the shape of Anarchism and Nepotism.

Laxmi Narayan

# FOREWORD / PREFACE

"By all accounts it has to be admitted that the book is a brave attempt to portray the malaise which in the land of Vivekananda and Gandhi, has gripped not merely the administrative machinery but the society as well. The author has given instances galore why his soul feels so tormented. Also laudable is his compassion for the silver haired and passion for providing hours for the elderly. However, the task of fulfilling this onerous task could be a daunting one since the Government, as also countrymen have not still realized the gravity of the problem – more so because the population of those who are 80 years or more belong to the fastest growing sector.

Curiously, the book is titled **"Evolution of Human Beings and Society"** which would have interested the Darwinians and Socialists since the book does not appear to discuss this aspect.

However, it may be said en passant that it is believed that for 1000 million years, the earth had no life and man appeared on the scene still millions of years later after the apes, the monkeys and there likes appeared on the stage.

The book is an outpouring of a disillusioned heart. How I wish that more Indians like **Shri Laxmi Narayan** could feel the pangs of the deprived and could raise their voices against the arrogance of the administration and the apathy of the Society. What is no less disturbing is his sad and unhappy relation with some members of his family which has added fuel to his agony."

**Neepesh Chandra Talukdar, IAS (Retd.), retired Member of Posts and Telegraphs Board, Government of India. New Delhi.**

MAHASVETA DEVI
GD-30 Rajdanga Main Road
Narkelbagan, Kolkata - 700107
Phone : (033) 2441 0408

I have read very eagerly the Book- **"Evolution of Human Beings and Society"** written by Sri Laxmi Narayan. Writer's explaining power and wide thinking is highly commendable. My self-filling and strength of mind express that this Book should reach to all libraries in villages and cities especially to the society of young generation.

With Best wishes,
Mahasveta Devi
**07.12.2011**

# PART - I

## SB'S LEARNING FROM VARIOUS BOOKS OF GREAT PHILOSOPHERS

1. **"The History of Dialectical Materialism"** written by **Dr. Che-Guevara:** This book reveals the evolution of human beings and society. When this earth has become cool and living life is being formed in amoeba, a single living cell in water and thereafter million and million years of changes/alienation from a single cell to various living creatures like fishes, birds, animals etc. later on further evolution and alienation from the above creatures and animals, human beings are arrived.

The further regeneration of intellectual human beings happened, when a man and a woman get together with heart and soul made an incident of accidental life product in chemical form in the womb of woman and take shape of human being who comes out after normal period of 9 or 10 months in the earth as rational animal. Human beings are rational animals having rationality and animality, whereas animal posses only animality. From this, we can understand our origin in the earth due to our father and mother and they are to be worshiped as our nearest God. Scientist, **Darwin** &

Economist/social analyst, **Karl Marx** believe, human beings by their intellect make the evolution of human beings and their society but not by God. **Mahatma Gandhi** said, "God/Ishwar/Allah Tero Naam Sabko Sanmati De Bhagwan". **Sri Ramkrishna Paramahanshadev** said God/Ishwar/Allah all are same as Water/Jal/Pani etc., these are only the change of names. This God, Ishwar, Allah in different names and different religion created by human beings who attained super power, really exists in the human brain and mind. In our Hindu Shastras this super power has been given different form of images for different power. 'Vishnu' is the 'Supreme Power, creator' of entire 'Brahmanda' i.e. 'Universe' and thereafter 'Vishnu' created number of Gods and Goddesses like 'Brahma', 'Shiva', 'Maa Durga', 'Maa Kali' etc with different powers on different times and in different places. And thereafter incarnation of all these Gods and Goddesses appeared in this earth with Super Power by their **Works, Prayers, Dhyanas, Yogas etc.** like **Shri Rama, Shri Krishna, Shri Gadadhar (Saint Ramakrishna Paramahanshadev), Shri Guru Nanak, Shri Goutam Buddha, Shri Mahavir/ Parashnath** and many other saints in Hindu religion, Jesus in Christian religion, Hazarath Mohamed in Islam religion etc.

2. **"Bharat Darshan"** by **Swami Vivekananda** is a big volume of philosophy on the evolution of human beings and society but unfortunately, it is now out of publication. Ramkrishna Mission has published a new book, which comprises of 8 volumes of **Swami Vivekananda's** works. We all are aware that our own Indian Hindu Culture, which Saint Shri Ramakrishna Paramhanshadev has revived, and Shri Swami

Vivekananda's work has become a commercial product under the control of foreign countries for earning profit. Possessing the works of our great philosophers and saints', the World Kings of capitalistic societies have built up a very big business organization in our country through which they earn money investing their capital and pick up all selected intellectuals from our country. If they do not get predominance entry in the business fields of our country, they will increase their sanctions to our neighboring countries to create disturbances in our border area.

In **'Bharat Darshan'**, **Swami Vivekananda** explained that the administration of a human society is run by a leader/ master on the basis of division of labours of different works namely:-

A) The tasks of **'Saints/Fathers'/Brahmins'/Gurus'/ Moulabis'** are to impart teachings **of gnyana (Knowledge)** to all. These **Saints/Fathers /Brahmins/ Gurus/ Moulabis** were the first ruler in the society when people were completely dependent on nature and were still trying to rule the society by their **Religious Fundamentalists** as God's Representatives. In ancient times devotees worshipped **God/Ishwar/Bhagwan/ Allah** as per the advice of **"Saints/Fathers/Brahmins/Gurus/ Moulabis"** to keep control of all natural calamities and to extract all needs from natural resources in land region and in water region. Therefore the ruling classes like Saints/Father**/ Brahmins/Gurus/Moulabis/Kings/Samrats/Badshahs / Jamindars" and there after Political Parties/Business Communities /Industrialists etc.** are utilizing all religious rules, norms, and methodology as instruments/weapons which working as opium to make all human beings as God-fearing creatures. In addition, all these Religious Fundamentalism created active enmity between one of religions with other religious believers. Government should include the religious philosophy in Education to develop the human mind and knowledge to keep people away from evil works. Spiritual gurus through their spiritual powers achieved through Yogas, Dhyanas, and Meditations create all the images of Gods and Goddesses. All crazy people observe the worship of all those Gods and Goddesses universally in general on the Road or in the Park. Due to this crazy entertainment, people are indulging:

1) Pollution in the atmosphere;
2) wastage of electrical consumption,
3) indiscipline crazy entertainment is the main cause of impediment of constructive works due to loss of man- hours. Government should stop these sorts of universal worship of all Gods and goddesses created by human beings. In addition, worship holidays should be limited for only one day.

**B) 'Khatryas'/Warriors** whose works are to protect the country and all human beings from enemies. Slowly it is observed that these **Khatryas** have become the rulers as **King** in any society.

**C) Baishyas/Businessmen,** whose responsibility is to provide things through barter system and/or money media for human beings in the society? Systematically these **Baishyas/**

**Businessmen** started controlling the entire economy and trying to capture the ruling power through their representatives as political parties to become richer over the poorer from Sudras and working classes.

**D) Sudras/Workers** are the ones who perform all various works like cleanliness and other various activities/works for all human beings in the society. These **Sudras / Workers** are becoming poorer; they may revolt for making **'Proletariat Dictatorship'** to rule the Society. **All these four divisions of labours are categorized as 'Caste'.**

According to **Swami Vivekananda,** these four divisions of labours, rule the society in cyclic order. Presently the **Baishyas/ businessmen** are financially rich in the capitalistic form of society, competent to utilize all the resources of the earth in a competitive way in qualitative and quantitative pattern, and rule the society. When the resources will be exhausted, rich will become richer and all other castes will become poorer. In addition, they will revolt and will capture the society for making a society under **Proletariat Dictatorship.** Other teachings of **Swami Vivekananda** from eight volumes of complete works – **"Yoga,"** which he explains through one symbol/logo of Ramakrishna Mission consisting of:-

   i)   **'Sun' shining as 'Gnyan Yoga'**
   ii)  **'Kundalini of Snake as 'Vakti Yoga'**
   iii) **'Wave'- as 'KarmaYoga'**
   iv)  **'Lotus on which a duck has taken place as 'Raj Yoga'**

**Swami Vivekananda** said that in any Yoga human beings could achieve the **'Moukshya'**. **SB** has chosen **'Karma Yoga'** but shifting in Kolkata permanently, he has become invalid and a worst victim of **'Extreme Self-Motivation'** developed in the society under the control of political parties' dictatorship. In this present scenario, people have lost their morality, honesty and humanity for the sake of achieving monetary gain by any means with unfair way.

If people study any of the religious books written by any and/or every **guru, saint, moulabi etc**. they would find that there are messages for people to live in peace with human considerations. However, many people with vested- interests who can be named as religious fundamentalists changed the application method in order to keep their dictatorship, and thus rule the society and keep it under their control.

**SB** finds that the women culture has changed. Women do not believe in **Sanatan Dharma** when they become self-sufficient. They do not foresee the respect they get in **Sanatan Dharma**. Children do not believe in the administration of their parents when they become adult and they are capable of managing themselves. **Sanatan Dharma** comes into existence in the society with both man and woman and extreme self-motivation will lead to separation and tensions in the rest of the life.

3. **"Red Book"** written by **Mao Tse Tung** is now banned everywhere in the entire world. This book says, "The Power comes from a barrel of a Gun". In India, the Naxalite, the Originator, **CM**, adopted to destroy the present state of affairs controlled by **Bourgeois** through destruction. The thinking

of grasping others' belongings by force and cheating method has developed in the minds of 99 per cent of the people as they do not have any kind of national feeling. Another aspect in the **"Red Book"** is **'Cultural Revolution'** to make successful communistic pattern of society. Cultural Revolution is required for controlling demand of individual requirements as well as of the society by way of heavy publicity or by law.

4a)  Now **SB** feels that it is high time to see that the society is administered by elected people in blocks, wards, parishads and districts. Political parties to unite people under one shed of certain manifests/philosophy to make people to live in peace and prosperity.

b)  **SB's** findings: Hardly 1 per cent of the political leaders are honestly thinking for the state and for the country. Some of the parties are billionaire by collecting money from people, business persons, and industrialists and by force on any occasion. They never follow the Government's circular that receipts and payments more than Rs.20, 000/- should be by cheque.

c)  **SB** feels that these unaccounted sources of income within the control of some leaders of all political parties would bring the Indian economy in a disastrous position if not controlled immediately. Moreover, the entire accounting system should be under scrutiny as per the Income Tax Law and it publishes publicly.

d) Government must have arrangement with all Foreign Banks authorities to know the total deposits of all Indians in all foreign Banks, which they are utilizing in investments for earning profit.

e) Government by law should make one constitution to elect, to employ and to select proper competent leaders on yearly basis for the maintenance of the day-to-day affairs with scheduled rights and powers for all human beings in blocks and in districts as well. **SB** assures that by this self-government system in blocks and districts where some power crazy groups creating terrorism to capture the present Government machineries to rule the society under their control and their demand for separate state for their own development could be set right with peace and in humanitarian grounds.

f) Reservation should be limited to OBC's and women only. OBC should include all castes and minorities. However, all these reservations to be selected from two categories of the people i.e. 70 per cent of sons of the soil and 30 per cent of the other people.

g) Any kind of organization is generally be administered by the Memorandum and Articles of Association. However, our Government administers the country through the constitution and by law. It is definitely advisable that the Assembly House and Parliament House should learn to maintain discipline and peaceful atmosphere in the meetings. On a smaller scale in any emergency services, there should not be any union by the employees supported by any political party, which creates disturbances in the form of slogans, processions, strikes, hooliganism with the intention to stop the work and get full salary without doing any work.

h) As usual most of the employees do not work for 8 hours. They kill the time by playing cards in the computer, and or reading newspapers, or gathering in canteen or elsewhere for many types of discussions. These sorts of activities are visible in many of the Government Offices. And if Government adopts private companies' system of granting employees' increments, bonus, incentive/exgratia, promotion etc. as per the parameter of their performance as recorded in the daily disposal report signed by employees and counter signature by the superiors with remarks. Then only efficiency in the government departments could be restored.

i) When country's partition took place due to religious fundamentalism and partition/migration caused huge loss of innumerable lives and many people migrated leaving their properties in order to save their lives by taking shelter in Relief and Rehabilitation Camps in other places. In addition, even after partition and fencing of the Line of control by Pakistan, Bangladesh and India, the influx of minorities from Pakistan and Bangladesh has never stopped. Some of our political parties have taken this influx as human assets for their Vote Bank to get 2/3$^{rd}$ majority in the general election and to keep the party's dictatorship intact in the society. The migrants in India from other neighbouring countries treat as second category of citizens without giving voting right.

j)  Everyone should approach the elected Nagarik Committee for the matter of sponsoring their appeal or petition to any Government Department and to the Judicial Department for avoiding delays, harassments, and monitory losses instead of submitting them through the agents, brokers, counselors, solicitors. All these agent brokers, counselors, solicitors should be appointed by the Nagarik Committee.

k)  In the Constitution, Nagarik Committee should collect fees directly as per the merit of the appeal from the people for giving required services for the settlement of concerned people's appeal. Nagarik Committee will deposit all these fees in the local banks and should be accounted on daily basis and audited quarterly. For the election of Leader/Head, application or nomination paper mentioning full particulars of the applicant/candidate and his knowledge of political, legal, administrative system to be ensured with detailed declaration and oath of the appropriate leaders and not by any recommendations from any political party.

l)  The State of West Bengal needs a competent and dynamic leader like Dr. B. C. Roy who could influence the Centre to promote the state's welfare. Government should be careful being the representative of major Political Party having maximum number of MPs to eliminate domination tendency by outside state leaders whose intentions are to destroy our economy. Here Constitution should be the supreme but not the Party. By this local self-government system, we can maintain peace without interference of police, slogans, processions, indiscipline attitude in the society.

m)  By the local self-government system, people can build up their own **SENA BAHINI** on pay rolls block/word-wise under the control of the Centre. Employees need Trade Unions in any industry/business organization under the control of local self-government for the control of maximum profit earning motive. This **SENA BAHINI** should be engaged in industry/ business organization as 'Trainee' to keep control of emergency services if any one goes for strike or lockout position.

n)  The elected Nagarik Committee should try to construct one development centre, one medical centre and one educational institution in every block to give compulsory education classes to all children and medical facility to all. The State Government should arrange finance taking the help from the Millionaires/ Billionaires.

o) Medical Centre in every Block must have reservation facility to all hospitals for emergency admission for BPL category people and for Senior Citizens with 50% discount in all treatments such as operation, all Laboratory Tests, medicines etc. Presently medicines costs increased almost double due to increase of commission to doctors by distributors for prescribing their medicines for long period. **SB** has become the worst victim while treatment under the doctors of one private Hospital near jadavpur T.B. Hospital and under any specialists attending any medical shops and in any Nursing Home with high rate visit charge. Earlier all doctors used to prescribe for 5 days or ten days for normal diseases of respiratory system, stomach, skin etc. Now they prescribe for one month to 3 months listing medicines of high rated new products, which are not available in Hospital's medicine shop, and patient has to buy from outside market @ **MRP** price. There after distributors will make a call to patient from where he has purchased those medicines or will visit patient house to check those medicine before paying doctor's commission. In every prescription doctor will prescribe for various laboratory tests, which at all not required and will advise to conduct the tests in their scheduled laboratory from where they get another commission.

p) Any person who intends to live in the society on ownership basis or on rental basis should approach the Nagarik Committee first to register his name so that he can live in peace.

q) This local self-government can even help the State Government and the Central Government by passing on various statistics of economical growth in the society including any fraudulent transactions by few people to accumulate unaccounted sources of income, which creates imbalance in the economic structure. If the Government makes one exclusive confidential Investigation Cell under the control of **CM** of the State, he/she can find all irregularities in all departments functioning under the Home Ministry, Finance Ministry, and other departments.

r) Huge turnover under the control of Transport Ministerial Departments for issuing licenses to all private bus owners, taxi owners and auto owners should be withdrawn for making all those transports under Government control to make the

City pollution free and which, ensures smooth journey for the people.

s) Another huge turnover under the control of Abasan Ministerial Department through whom so called Business Community is looting public money for giving flats on extraordinary high rates in West Bengal. **SB** himself witnessed one offered place in ......... where vacant land fenced by M/s ..... with offer price of Rs.1600/- per sq. ft. approximately was so high on built up area but actual carpet area will be less by 25 percent then the actual price will become Rs.2000/- approximately. Almost all real estate companies have partnership with the earlier Government controlled by Party-King, Dictator. After ruling for more than three long decades continuously the said Party–King could not arrange to own a Real Estate Construction Company to provide affordable residential units to **LIG**, **MIG** and **HIG** people as per their capacity.

t) All departments have syndicate between all staff members to collect extra money in cash for clearing any matter, disputes and sanction. **SB** himself had to pay huge money in cash directly and/or through agents to the following Departments:-

1) Kolkata Municipal Corporation, people named **(Chorporation).**

2) **BLRO** for mutation

3) Police Station for executing court orders I.O. collects 'Kharcha-Pani' in cash from both the parties Complainant and Opponent directly and/or through

Advocate, Agent, Broker, acting counseling but charge -sheet would be in favour of who pays more money with the consent of the Officer-In-Charge. All hawkers have to pay to police to keep their occupied place for installing temporary shops and/or making sale of product on trolley on the roadside.

u) To build up any industry/project one requires capital, machinery, technical expertise and man power but for the destruction, only ego and man power is required.

v) When a State runs through anarchism under the control of political party's dictatorship, people should unite and declare indefinite strike till president's rule is imposed for fresh election from block to district level for forming a new Government including self local Government.

5. According to comrade Lenin, to make strong position, a Party should merge with other nearest strong opposition groups to become self sufficient physically, economically, politically and in all respects instead of attacking that strong opposition groups as imperialist. Parties should learn from China that before making the society under proletariat dictatorship, it should first become capitalist and this is the cyclic order as per Swami Vivekananda. In addition, there is another chapter of Comrade Lenin's works, according to which parties should make self-criticism for their mistakes in the process of struggle.

6. **Judicial Department:-** Mostly all junior or senior advocates collect their fees in cash from clients but decline to give any

receipt for the same and then think of their I.T. Return. By law, they should maintain a register for taking any amount of fee from the clients mentioning the case details, names and addresses of clients. Stamp vendors charge more cash than the tender value from the purchaser other than advocates. Unauthorized vendors are charging more than the authorized vendors. By law, they also should maintain a register for issuing stamps and other judicial papers mentioning price and details of stamps along with the customers' signatures. The judges' judgment differs on cash settlement. All subordinate staffs of any court collect cash for allowing the files to be read and giving Xerox of any report of any petitioner party. Everywhere unaccounted source of income has created imbalance in the economy. Government must bring some amendments of Criminal Procedure Code and the Civil Procedure Code to give justice to the bonafide Complainant in limited time-period instead of hanging around for unlimited years without justice and/or to give some relief for survival when some cases are prolonging for long period. Some times when there are intense arguments between the advocate and the judge on any particular case for not arranging any hearing date for more than two years, judge gives next attendance date after 8 months. In Consumer Disputes Redresal Forum, any case normally takes 6 to 7 hearings but due to mal-practices of advocates, namely, resort to absenteeism, non-submission of requisite documents or statements, the case continues for more than a year so that the advocates on both the sides can claim their attendance fees. Everywhere you will find sign of anarchism.

7. **Price Index:** If Government accepts production under 'liaise-fare' system, distribution and price should be under Government control. This we can execute through elected Nagarik Committee by law as per statistical data of demand and supply ratio. Every product should be on **MRP** rate chart basis and we should not allow millionaire/billionaire companies to procure any product directly from the farmers and manufacturers to create artificial shortage in the market due to monopoly tendency. Value of money lies in circulation of money. We should avoid keeping surplus hard cash in house as dead assets, instead we should invest in the money market or deposit in the banks as Fixed Deposits. We can achieve maximum profit through maximum volume of sales by reducing sale price slightly to increase the demand for the increase of purchasing capacity. Profit margin should not be more than 10 per cent to the producers and to the wholesalers and retailers while calculating **MRP Price** of any industrial products. In addition, maximum 100 percent for agricultural products produced only once in a year by farmers but wholesalers or retailers should not claim more than 10 per cent.

We all are aware that natural resources are limited and almost more than 80 per cent within our reach already extracted and processed for human consumption through industrial and technical support. However, population increases very rapidly, therefore, difference between demand and supply increases immensely. **SB** feels processing cost should remain stand still like in China, who adopted controlling method of human demand as per **"RED BOOK".** Their personal cost is very low than ours. Our personal cost increases every moment on demand from Trade Union and political parties. When they do strike and shout slogan resulting in loss of man works and further increase of price of all essential commodities as well. Over and above moneylenders, keep money in advance with the farmers to collect immediately when the farmers cut off the agricultural products and hand over to the lender in lower price and lender sells to wholesaler in Mandis or in go-downs with maximum profit. There after the wholesaler manipulates by hoarding in secret and creates artificial shortage for increasing the price when the demand increases. If government enforces through sales tax and income tax department to investigate all Mandis and go-downs and all wholesalers' offices and residences, they can get the key of controlling Price Index.

**SB** feels increase of price index arises due to **liaise fare System** and introduction of **"Globalization"** with no control and unlimited democratic right. All industrialists, business people, professionals are in a warpath to make maximum profit with no limit. General people are also in the same run to make money by cheating, looting, forgetting honesty and humanity. Due to this globalization, all Government Departments are very badly affected by the influence of huge money inflow under the table from business communities and general people for getting immediate license, permit etc., and in addition political parties are putting pressure to the government through their respective unions for the increase of basic salary of employees to capture their votes. Government may also fulfill their demands by increasing the supply of money through extra printing of notes.

There should be immediate ordinance that basic rate should not be changed from the fixed rate as per the category.

Only D.A. as per the monthly average changes in Price Index would affect in the monthly pay, which should be either way if price index goes down. From profit, employees are entitled to get production bonus, exgratia, incentives etc. for their extra ordinary individual contribution in the organizations, institutions and all establishments. Another Ordinance is also required removing all unions from all emergency services provided by companies, organizations, institutions etc. under the control of Government and/or Private. Special Tribunal will settle all disputes/demands of all employees in stipulated time. Employees should not cease their work by using their power of strike or 'work to rule' systems. Severe punishment may impose iceasing their pay under the control of military governance. In this ordinance, following categories of services are to be included in emergency service categories namely food, water, electricity, health, education, conveyance, transportation on land, sky and in water; telecommunications and all bank operating systems.

No democratic right will be entertained to stop these emergency services. In the military governance, we require experienced personnel to handle all the departments of emergency services, and for which we will make mass recruitments from all district level considering reservation only from OBC and Women on merit. and thereafter from general categories for training in the respective departments as a post of 'Trainee' on temporary basis with a fixed monthly allowance according to their qualification, experience and capability. In future, they will be absorbed in the department as and when required, permanently under the control of military governance. By this, consistency in economical growth will remain as it is. We must know that the economical theories written by all noble laureates and highly qualified experts' opinions are only applicable in developed countries but not for developing country like ours. To keep the industrial and economical growth in upward position, government should impose 20% infrastructure development tax on net profit quarterly basis from all establishments and all individual millionaires /billionaires under government control or private control for development of basic amenities in the societies and uninterrupted emergency services mentioned above for all people in block label to district label. And if **liaise-fare' system and globalization** with no control will make **80% BPL & APL Categories of People's** condition in calamitous position.

How our Billionaires are donating billions of Rupees in other Developed Countries for their Research and Development instead why they should not donate in their own country. To develop their generosity 20% Tax should be imposed and new license for New Industry their investment should include Research Centre, own Power Plant and other infrastructures for employees' developments. Countries 80% people are living in village side and 20% in City area. Industrial and Business growth in City creates jobs and village people are rushing in City. Whereas through local **Self Government System** we can set up Agricultural based Small Scale Industries and job oriented business development if our Government adopt Micro Finance System of Noble Laureate, **Dr. Mohd. Yunus**, we can create jobs for all village people instead of providing 100 days jobs for few people. It is deception by disguise to the village poor people. However, we must be careful to select proper executive elected members.

Before choosing any one for a position for promotion, we should obtain Bond and Affidavit from every one which will be the profile and guarantee of individual to maintain clear and clean services for people of the Block/Word in the District. We know that 99% people in the present society are vitiated directly or indirectly for own personal extra gain. Land acquisition Act, for new Industries and our own Infrastructure projects like Road, Light, Water and other various projects required to be changed in such a way, that Government need not spend from existing Budget Fund.

**First: Land acquisition for new Industry:**

1.  Industrialist should be prepared to pay land price as per landowner's demand,
2.  Rehabilitation of Land owner's family including service to the capable members of the family,
3.  Infrastructure development cost to be reimbursed to the Government in advance immediately after registration. **Second: Development Project:** Government should arrange Contractor on joint venture agreement @ 50/50 ratio. Revenue earned from the Project will be shared 55/45 ratio. 55% for Government and 45% for Contractor for 10 years terms then the entire project automatically will remain with the Government only.

We all are aware that if we do not give preoccupancy of Business Communities and Industrialists of World King in our country on globalization system we will not be able to keep our economical and industrial growth intact and lack of growth will affect the Price Index immensely. However, we should invite them on 40% to 49% **FDI** right only without violating our fundamental and human right. If we allow them more than 50%, investment right then our country's economy will be under their control.

Government may try to reduce corruption within members of parliament and assembly by increasing their pay scale, instead **SB** feels there should be pension scheme if any member completing minimum 5 years terms or alternatively social service according to individual capacity on payroll and if senior citizen, should provide **"Old age Home"** under government control.

If we keep on increasing only government employees pay scale then what about rest of people from more than 126 Crores people of this country. How we will control price index?

Government should try to revive all closed industries under the control of **BIFR** and by taking the help of old employees as Coparcener with profit sharing ratio.

At the end, **SB** feels that when there is a Minimum Wages Act, then why we should not introduce Maximum Wages Act to make limit of reasonable maximum salary. As per information and record some business persons and industrialists are drawing salary in billions rupees and there after billions of rupees profit on investment and others are starving. Pay Commission Report for increasing salary should declare redundant when D.A. is compensating the Price Index.

Resources are limited and population is increasing but few people's pay pockets are overflowing with corruption method. How Price Index will be under control?

**SB** used to travel by rail to Mumbai twice in a month for closing of his old establishments. In the year 2006/07 one day he asked the pantry supervisor to produce the bill for vegetable meal. That supervisor was scared and could not produce any bill. Then **SB** asked for complaint book and finally the supervisor produced item wise bill of Rs.45/- which should be Rs.35/- flat rate. Panir Cutlet costing Rs.22/- was out of Menu. Even though the cost was high but unfortunately in that cutlet **SB** could not find any crunches of Panir, and it was like a vegetable cutlet. When **SB** challenged and asked for Complaint Book, the supervisor apologized and offered him VIP treatment without any charges. However, **SB** refused and paid the money. When **SB** asked supervisor why they are charging so much for providing bad quality of food, supervisor replied that in order to get this railway catering contract, they had to pay separate 'cash packet' for getting the contract. Presently Food Contractors' rate has become so high that **80% APL & BPL** categories people can not afford. Veg. Plate charging Rs.80-/ and Non Veg Plate charging Rs.100/-. If we ask for Bill they will produce itemwise rate not **IRCTC** Thali rate and they will not supply Pot Tea of Rs.7/- They will charge Rs.10/-of one cup. Even if you travel now by Rajdhani Express, it is observed by anyone that the meal items were reduced as compared to the catering when it was under direct control of Railway Board. In the platform or in the compartment all food items including tea and coffee supplied at a very high rate and quality is poor as compare to the supplies available from outside the railway station premises.

At the end, people can remember that the politically educated leaders had expressed their thought to run and administer this united sub continent initially by military rulers and thereafter under Presidential form of government to make this country a perfect democratic country. Because everybody knew it that the opportunists and self centered power crazy leaders would capture the entire administration of this country for their own interests taking advantages of peoples' poverty, lack of proper education and discipline. Everybody knew that there were one extreme self centered power crazy group and other one religious fundamentalists group, and both were much closed pets of the **Father of the Nation**, **Sri Mahatma Gandhi** from whom they managed to take sanction of dividing the country into two parts. And the result of which the Father of the nation had to leave the country for ever for heaven. Later on, different opportunists', revolutionary group started capturing the entire government machineries to rule this state by destroying the existing industries through their trade unions for making new construction. In addition, one group of extreme revolutionaries for mass destruction for capturing power as per slogan of **Mao Tse Tung** that **"Power comes from a Barrel of a Gun"**. Moreover, some people have become terrorists with the help of foreign collaboration to fulfill their religious fundamentalism and power crazy mentality. At least, affected places of few states under the control of terrorists, Government should declare under emergency military rule immediately.

After independence all self centered power crazy dirty politicians took the reign of our country by adopting Mount Batten policy of 'divide and rule' keeping alive racial difference, casteism and religious fundamentalism to rule this democratic country in the shape of **ANARCHISM**. These dirty politicians when require can declare emergency on created war to keep their power intact. There is one book written by **Dr. Nirod Chandra Chowdhury** regarding untold story of Chinese aggression from which we find that the War is created and then retreat. The history of betrayal of First King of Democratic Sub-Continent.

When the above Self Centered Party-King, Dictator destroyed the West Bengal State and new Party-King took the reign of this State in all respects through their cadres, leaders and trade unions. And there after some of their leaders are enjoying 'Z' securities after making their kith and keen as established Industrialists and business persons. Moreover, after demise they may get country's highest farewell with 21-gun salute honour for their long association in dirty politics. The **Noble laureate, Rabindra Nath Tagore** had written our National Anthem **"JANA GANA MANA ADHINAYAKA................."** to commemorate the visit of **Mahatma Gandhi** whom he recognized as the only one national **Nayak** in the country when visited in his **Shanti Niketan Ashram.**

There after self-centered Power Crazy Opportunists had captured the power of this state in the Shed of Party-King. These Party King should construct **VIP Bridhyashrams** to keep their senior leaders secured instead of providing 'Z' security to save the public money. Above all, it may further be noticed that some leaders will construct their own permanent images, when they will be chief administrator of any State or of the Country, in the park or on any national platform to make people to start worshiping them as Gods.

Now we should try to make leaders from block level but not from the party to bring back the national feelings among the people.

# Part - II

## STORY OF 'SB' (SUKUMAR BANERJEE) WHO HAS LANDED IN MISERIES AFTER SHIFTING TO KOLKATA IN HIS PARENTAL HOUSE FOR CONSTRUCTION OF OLD-AGE-HOME/BRIDHYASHRAM

Witnessing the present scenario in city life, joint family structure has been demolished due to self-motivation developed in the minds of all individuals in the family; as a result, the relation in the family has become a business relation. Moreover, all blood relations among husband, wife, father, mother, son, daughter, brother, sister have become superfluous. Parents bring up their children from motionless position to self-sufficient position as per their duty and above all for the sake of humanity. Nevertheless, when those parents become old and become incapable to move comfortably, children do not feel the necessity of giving them relief. In fact children are separated from the parents and do not bother even to enquire about the parents' condition. It is steel happening that due to below poverty condition some people torture their own children by using filthy languages and sometimes even beat their wives with shoes in front of others for not getting money from their wives' parents' houses.

**SB** is strongly of the view that establishment of **Old-Age-Home/** (**BRIDHYASHRAM**) is necessary. And **SB** has decided to construct a **"Bridhyashram** for senior citizen" who can be considered as condemned **'APARTHEID'** in the modern society**,** to give comfortable, secured peaceful life with the following facilities:-

1. Room with attached W.C. & Bathroom on rental and Lease basis.
2. Nursing facility for all on reasonable rate
3. Small clinic with chemist's shop and physiotherapy arrangements on meager rate.
4. Telecommunication facility with interconnected auto telephones.
5. Departmental shopping facility at reasonable rate
6. Availability of ambulances on emergency basis for admission in big hospitals and confirmation of prearranged beds to be ensured by donation of one time subscription by life members and fees from ordinary members
7. Apart from this, Health Club on the roof of the building for life members and ordinary members with lift facility up to 3$^{rd}$ Floor on monthly chargeable basis for the following:-

   a) Morning walk,
   b) Laughter Yoga centre,
   c) Badminton and Table Tennis

    d)   Library with reading facility

8.   This **BRIDHYASHRAM** is a non profitable Organization and to be functional as per actual cost Plus 10 per cent for maintenance and reserve fund

9.   There are some old people living alone in a rented Flat or in is/her own Flat with anxiety if he/she become sick, for such people we can give shelter in our **BRIDHYASHRAM** taking their Flat in our possession.

10.  Security Guard, Cleaning, Nursing etc. will be provided on monthly chargeable basis from each occupants including 10% service charges on actual.

11.  At the time of construction, local people will get job. One day **SB** was dreaming in the middle of the night that Kolkata has become beautiful, peaceful and pollution-free resulting from the following initiatives. To make Kolkata free from road jam and congestion due to hawkers, we must give boot contract to any foreign expert for multi storied international bus terminal from basement to Second Floor creating the following facilities:

A)  Basement will be for Inter State/Inter District Buses.
B)  Ground floor will be for local Buses.
C)  First Floor will be for hawkers.
D)  Second Floor will be for meeting of all Political Parties, International Book Fairs etc. under open sky.

These terminals should have facility of providing snacks, tea, fast food, toilet and bathrooms, maintenance workshop including oil and lubricants supply. For the above-mentioned plan, following are the two places available:-a) Entire Esplanade area and Babu Ghat Area and secondly, b) One few acres open plot earmarked for **'Bridhyashram'** as per local peoples' report attached with Eastern by-pass Road near Mukundapur. These two terminals can remove all hawkers from South Kolkata, Central Kolkata, and North Kolkata areas. The **'Boot'** (Build, Own, Operate and Transfer) contractors can build these two terminals on their own cost for themselves and operate to earn revenue as per 60/40 ratio for 10 years and there after transfer them to the Local Government.

Another jam in Jadavpur Station Road and Jadavpur P.S. and Prince Anwar Shah Road Crossing can be removed by constructing a fly over-cum-shopping mall on the both sides for small dealers and all vehicles across the rail crossing and from South Sukanto Setu to Jadavpur P.S. junction towards East West Anwar Shah Bridge and Eastern bypass. And in this flyover metro rail also can be added. This also can be given on a Boot Contract to the Foreign Expert.

All railway lines passing through city can be covered with fly over for rehabilitation of slum dwellers and hawkers. In addition, all these infrastructure projects can be given on **'Boot'** Contract again to Foreign Experts.

Another sensitive area:-North Kolkata, including Burabazar Area should be declared a National Heritage City. Possibly this area has become the shelter of all corrupt and smugglers who are famously known as businesspersons from Burabazar. If we open the history of 19th century's Bengal renaissance, we will find all our great educationists, philosophers, men of literatures, artists, revolutionists and freedom fighters used to reside in this area and were fighting for the freedom of our country. Especially when we see the birth place of our great noble laureate**, Rabindra Nath Tagore**, which should have been an international tourist place, has become nauseating sight in this area after independence under control of self centered power crazy dirty politicians.

**SB** remembers one incidence when he had visited Bakkhali fish breeding aquarium where sea water and sweet water mixed, number of ponds are excavated for fish breeding. Incidentally **SB** asked one fisher man, about the total income from all these ponds in a year, who could not reply but one thing he told that 50% ownership, belongs to Mr. Chandan Bose by name. **SB** feels there should be CBI enquiry to find out total expenditures of this partnership project borne by what ratio. From Howrah station to Burabazar area, after ferry crossing and Howrah Bridge crossing over River Ganga, all smuggled goods are possibly being stored in this area. Entire business community people have captured this entire North Kolkata area. These business communities have become the main money suppliers to the King-Party and are ruling this State. The complete economy is under their control. In West Bengal, in respect of film industry they are the main financiers, who are forcing producers, directors to make movies of low grade to earn maximum profit. State Government should take control of all go-downs, cold storages and should make local people as Co-Partner in their business and industries to control the distribution and price. We should shift this wholesale market somewhere near Eastern bypass area and/or Rajarhat area. We should demolish all old buildings including Old Scrapped Mint area and rebuild the Heritage City for international residential school and college for all branches of arts, commerce & science/technologies including management level for the fellow citizens on nominal fees and for international people on international standard. In these schools and colleges, we should inscribe all the works of all great people of West Bengal and other states who participated in their works staying in this area. These schools and colleges should follow the ideology of our illustrious person of literature, **Rabindra Nath Tagore** fully under the control of Centre. Next we should construct big hospitals for poor, tourist amusement park and shelter for foreigners and others. We can get foreign aid and expertise for remodeling this city. If we visit some foreign countries where any river is passing through city, we will find that both sides of the river bank has been utilized beautifully with garden, road, metro rail, transportation with number of bridges for crossing one stoppage to other stoppages. For developing all the above we can give **'Boot'** Contract on 40/60 ratio for Ten Years to clear off contractors' investments with profit.

## CONSTRUCTION OF BRIDHYASHRAM

Presently **SB** including his other two brothers has … sq. ft. plus…….. sq. ft. Western side of …... width road after release of …….. sq. ft. encroached by North & South side neighbours. If Nagarik Committee could convince all the neighbours from Purbachal Main Road to South Kalitala Road western side of the 9 ft. inside road widening up to 12 ft. for long stretch of roof, can convert all single stories and double stories building to third story building keeping their ownership intact without merging with each other on self promoting system. Only roof will be common for health club and ceremonial purposes. **SB,** being a joint promoter will invest capital for the development of the land and sanctioning the plan for construction of the said building, as per the registered agreement for construction on 60/40 ratio as mentioned below:-

The landowner and **SB** jointly will promote and execute the contract as per the registered agreement within the schedule time & price. Landowner would get complete FAR. **SB** would collect cost analysis from civil contractor and will prepare construction agreement, which would sign by self and landowner jointly with contractor. Then **SB** would make another agreement with Landowner for constructing the building on 60/40 ratio. Builder/Promoter will utilize 60% for Senior Citizens. At the time of construction and for running of **BRIDHYASHRAM** all the **BPL** family members can get jobs for earning their livelihood. At the time of construction, the landowner's family members need not shift immediately and will accommodate in the other constructed building for a short period. Security guard, cleaning/nursing will be provided on chargeable basis for services and maintenance on actual plus 10 per cent per flat. **SB** has submitted one note satisfying both the accused elder and younger brother for the settlement in the month of December'08. **Supriyo,** elder brother, who is **extreme self motivated destructive evil egoist,** did not accept any proposal. Builder/Developer would execute an agreement with **SB** for **'Boot' (Build, Own, Operate and Transfer)** Contract after completion of the project in all respect on 40/60 ratio. But all efforts became meaningless, because **Supriyo** whose character history is mentioned below, did not respond at all. Moreover, finding no alternative **SB** has to file criminal suit under sec.420 & 406 against the ...........................

After shifting permanently here in Kolkata, Parental House, **SB** has learned from two brothers during neighbours, younger brother, sisters and other relatives about the destruction history of **extreme self-motivated destructive evil egoist**, **his elder brother, Supriyo** after marriage separated from his father and there after his various ill treatments started towards the old father for the occupation of the land.

1) He has sold out Jadavpur Shop where **SB's** younger brother was working simply to makehim jobless without giving him any compensation.

2) Due to his change over from CPM to Naxalite group, his opponent group had thrown bomb on their father's bamboo cane Hutment was burnt into ashes and after that **Supriyo**, with his family shifted to Chandan Nagar.

3) Due to his wife and his instigation, their younger sister left the house and married inter-caste, a local boy and as a result, he got relief from spending any marriage expenses.

4) The opinion of the neighbours, and relatives was that **S**upriyo had killed his wife by not giving proper medical treatment.

5) Due to his self-motivation to save money his younger daughter also left house and married inter-cast, a local boy.

6) **Supriyo's** extreme self-motivation has thrown out his only one son from his house. As a result this young

boy started to live in a guest house and managed the expenses from the tuition he used to do and later on when he came to **SB**, in New Bombay, **SB** arranged job for him in the company, when he was working there as a Manager, Accounts and Taxation. Now **Supriyo's** son has become a self-sufficient married man and manages abroad assignments also.

7) After retirement, **Supriyo,** as per his statement he lost all of his savings in share market and could save Rs........../-for his elder daughter's marriage.

8) Due to short fall in marriage expenses he borrowed money from Ashok, husband of their younger sister but could not return and the result of which their sister had been thrown out by her husband. Their elder sister's husband gave that money to Ashok and managed to send back their younger sister to her husband's house. When their elder sister's husband asked for refund of the sum given, he was abused.

9) In the year 1973 by force **Supriyo** managed to make one 'Sales Deed' for .... l... sq. ft. of land, wherein their Bamboo Cane Hutment was burnt into ashes due to Bombing attack by **Supriyo's** opponent party when **Supriyo** became Naxalite from CPM party in the year 1971. The above Sales Deed was registered taking signature from their father with consideration of Rs......... shown as receipt in the deed without payment and constructed building on the said land encroaching some part from the balance......... sq. ft. of land. Next In the year ........., their father with fear made a gift deed for the balance ........... sq.ft. of

land in favour of **SB's** name & his younger brother's name thinking of elder brother's self motivated action may capture the whole land and he would throw out their younger brother and **SB's** entry in that land for ever. Father conveyed this to **SB** when he was in…….. in Gulf Country in the year…...

10) In the year ……. elder brother, **Supriyo** sold that land and building to Mr. Pinaki in Rs…….. out of which he promised to give share to two brothers when **SB** visited once in his house before selling that premises. And this whole amount also he lost in share market as per his statement, and did not pay two brothers' share.

11) Due to his illegal construction by encroaching gifted land on which **SB** cannot make any permanent construction on 13 ft. width remain out of 25 ft. length from South to North as the plan cannot be approved.

12) **SB** did approach to Mr. Pinaki, who purchased **Supriyo's** land and building, to construct further and requested to make amalgamation jointly of two lands together but he refused. **SB** did put up the complaint to KMC and on final hearing it was confirmed that the said building is in the demolition case and advised **SB** to file a suit to civil court and Mr. Pinaki was advised to take NOC from Corporation by paying penalty to go ahead for construction on the first floor. Nevertheless, elder brother's dirty politics made youngest brother, his puppet that refused to sign any suit paper or to give **SB** any power of attorney to file

a suit. Due to the above damages, elder brother owes compensation of Rs............ to both the brothers.

13) The secretary, Mr. Sudhir of the Local Nagarik Committee who had accumulated huge properties from unaccounted sources of income for a long period and when it was noticed by the party, he was asked to step down. New Local Committee Secretary, Mr. Abhisek also followed the predecessor's tactics to make his position strong and supported that new landowner, Pinaki and to **SB's** younger brother.

14) Now **Supriyo** made his next target to destroy **SB** by not allowing constructing the building on the plot **No.** ... & ... due to his unsuccessful attempt to get **SB's** signature on original **'Gift Deed'** prepared by **Supriyo**, elder brother on Rs.250/- non judicial stamp paper for occupying $1/3^{rd}$ share with one room structure from the premises No...... of........ sq.ft. of land with structure, which their father had gifted to **SB** and younger brother's name to prevent further encroachment by the eldest one, **Supriyo**. There is a rumar that this Supriya at the age of 73 again got married.

15) In the year.... 2004 onward **SB** started visiting Kolkata and met elder brother who declared that he has no interest, above all no money, no time, and he was to be considered as dead for doing anything further on the father's occupied.......... sq.ft. of Land. **SB** took all the original receipts and papers and visited Mrs. Bharati's house, land owner of the new land with elder brother and tempted her to give more money

and as a result **SB** gave one post dated cheque of Rs…….. to elder brother but Mrs. Bharati demanded Rs……….. And finally with the help of Advocate, Mr. Narayan, who could manage to get judgment from the Registrar of Assurance, Alipure Registrar Office to pay stamp duty and registration fees. **SB** did send all the Stamp duty and Registration fees from Mumbai to elder brother by registered post in covered letters twice. In the covering letters **SB** explained his purpose and intention to start a business for helping poor kith and keens and especially he wanted to give some money to his younger brother for trading business. Again, penalty clause introduced for time bar for non-registration in time. In 2004 **SB** arranged loan of Rs………… from Citi Bank card over telephone for paying ten times penalty of Rs………….. to complete the registration of the said new land by paying Rs…….. Monthly EMI and thus elder brother paid 13 installments @ Rs…….. per month. Since half of the money exhausted due to **SB's** hospitalization under elder brother's care, again **SB** took further loan from HDFC card which was sanctioned over the telephone and the amount was Rs……….. Which **SB** kept in a joint FD A/c in HDFC Bank, near Dumdum and opened a current A/c for O.D. facility in the name of himself with elder brother. But in the year…….. **SB** did close both the accounts. However, EMI of Rs…………. was paid by **SB** alone against HDFC Card. **SB** was engaged himself full time since…….. onward to recover the encroached land. **SB initially** started living in Kolkata with his elder brother for few days then put up in his parental House. And took up everything in his custody and started frequently going to Mumbai for arranging the finance and for closing 38 years old establishment and various bank loans and other pending court cases. Then finally came back to Kolkata permanently in the year........ **Supriyo** after the sale of his own constructed building he was residing in **SB's** present Room, wherein the incidence and accident occurred during his stay with younger Brother's wife. She, who tried to explained to **SB.** And later on **SB** had realized when **SB** was attacked and abused by his next neighbour, Pinaki and his wife using filthy language viz: "Haramjada to **SB** and "Khanki Magi" to Younger Brother's wife. **SB** has to write a letter to Pinaki for written apology. In addition, advised him to sale the wrong Constructed Building against which **SB** filed a case to KMC for demolition to avoid continuous quarrelling. Presently Elder Brother earning and living with Government Pension of about more than Rs......... P.M. and by teaching Junior classes students for which he is working so hard for developing his own teaching capacity day and night and got minor heart attack admitted in Railway's B. R. Singh Hospital.

16) Before leaving for Bombay in the month of .......... when **SB's** elder brother was in hospital **SB** wrote one letter and handed over it to him when he came back from hospital through Mr. Jaydeb, who lived with his elder brother in the mess. In that letter, **SB** requested

him to come back to their Parental House and allow **SB** to start building construction works. And further requested to sign the development agreement and power of attorney so that all could stay peacefully together and he could look after the construction instead of staying separately at this old age when nobody would be there if anything further happened.

17) For arranging further fund for development of the land and construction of new Building, **SB** has sent first flat booking receipt to his nephew, Bunty on his organization's letter head duly signed by two brothers with **SB** himself, owner of M/s BS Contracting and Services as civil contractor. In addition, thereafter all three brothers have signed another flat booking advance receipt on his organization's letterhead for borrowing money from his friend Shaik Shamim, business person,……., Maharastra.

Later on when **SB** requested both for power of attorney and development agreement to start construction for better living standard, elder brother stated, **"We don't believe you"**. Then **SB** wrote a letter and couriered to his elder brother **Supriyo**, which was received by his mess cook, which said:

**"THOUGHT OF CONSIDERATION FOR CONSTRUCTION AND THERE AFTER DESTRUCTION TAKES PLACE IMMEDIATELY <u>AFTER WHEN SOME ONE STATES, I DON'T BELIEVE YOU".</u>**

After the retirement, **SB's** younger brother for whom he did arrange a job in his company again in the year 1998, could not continue for long time and came back to Kolkata home after resigning in the year 2003. During this period, his younger brother was passing very bad time, and he used to give calls to **SB** frequently that all of his full and final savings were almost exhausted and cannot pull on for long time. And also gave calls to **SB** for saving their father's acquired land which was encroached and was going to be encroached fully from all the sites if **SB** did not take proper steps to save their father's acquired land.

**SB** took decision to shift to Kolkata and this decision of shifting also deteriorated the family relation which resulted in **SB** living alone in his .......... flat leaving his own purchased new flat in 15 Storied Millennium Tower which declared luxury apartment in..........., New Mumbai. **SB's** wife did not tolerate any member of his parent's family due to their inhuman tortures during the period of 2.1/2 months in the year......... when SB left for .......... in UAE for arranging visa to take the family.

During his stay in Kolkata since........ **SB** used to spend his single penny for completely of joint family expenditures when SB was staying with his younger brother jointly to give him indirect financial relief and later on arranged business loan from his O.D. Account with SBI.

Before **SB's** entry in his parental house, his younger brother who was working in Bangalore allowed his wife to rent one front Room & attached Varanda to his neighbor, Jiban's wife name for her son's family at Rs....... per month on Rs.10/- Stamp paper agreement with younger brother's wife, who was not an owner of this parental house. With great difficulty, **SB's** younger brother after returning Rs....... deposit and by touching Mrs. Jiban's feet did beg for the release of the two rented rooms.

Such a worst culture has developed in the society that everybody wants to grasp others' property by any means with the help of local strong people. Mr. Jiban had started attacking **SB** so that he might not think of settling down here and like there were other people including **SB's** old friends of his young age also started advising him to go back to Mumbai. Because he cannot stay here adjusting himself in the present culture developed in the area where his two brothers are also infected with this culture. The same younger brother joined with his eldest brother to oppose **SB** in all respect by taking ............ rupees from elder brother. In the year........ **SB did** arrange counseling in the Office of one retired judge M/s .......... & Co. inviting accused two brothers. When, counseling started the younger brother repeated the same promise that he would take care of elder brother, **Supriyo's** prestige and fame spoiled in connection with his wife, which was informed to **SB** by his elder brother, **Supriyo** with tears in his eyes due to the shock when **SB** visited his house.

In addition, same day **Supriyo** did agree to dispose of his ........ cottahs of land by Rupees......... except encroached portion in south side. After that **SB's** younger brother started propagating that their father was not willing to add **SB's** name in the **Gift Deed** when **SB** was in UAE. He further started telling that he made a mistake for allowing **SB** to enter in their Parental House. When **SB** made him so strong, powerful and such ungrateful brother that how he can deny through his learned advocate, Mrs. Maya, who informed **SB's** learned advocate, Mr. Narayan by registered post that his client had not taken any money from **SB** and did not permit to construct any building on the newly purchased and developed land. **SB** has given all the detailed statements of business loan to his younger brother and the Renovation expenses for the old hutment with full facility. And the next detailed statement of cost and expenses for recovering new land for which **SB's** younger brother has got no contribution but has become 1/3$^{rd}$ owner of the new land as his name has been included in the **Conveyance Deed**. When encroached land had become Vastu land from Shali land after completing BLRO & KMC mutation and with earth filling by **SB's** investment of Rupees……….. by taking banks loan and undergoing hardship, then everybody had become the owner of 1800 sq.ft. each from total Vastu land of…….. sq. ft. The elder brother, **Supriyo** had taken a stand to destroy **SB** and was obstructing him to construct a building on the said developed land so that **SB** could not recover his investment amount to clear his bank loan and to keep that land unutilized as dead asset.

Next **SB** had written a letter, to the Secretary, Mr. Sudhir of Nagarik Committee, signed by Asstt. Secretary, Mr. Nikhil, who kept that letter pending for 11 months and gave back to **SB** for the submission of the same to the office address, which **SB** further submitted in the beginning of 2008. The Nagarik Committee arranged meeting by calling both the brothers. On the hearing date the Asstt. Secretary, Mr.Nikhil had read the complain letter of **SB's** younger brother stating his complain had been received first than **SB's** complain letter which was factually received by him more than one year before and again placed further in the office in the month of .......'2008. In the meeting all LCM and Secretary, President were present and put their signature in the minutes register but the conclusion (Sidhyanta) was signed by the President instead of Secretary to whom the complaints had been submitted earlier. **SB** did receive Conclusion Report of Nagarik Committee after 7 days. Nagarik Committee's Conclusion Report stated that there will be no injustice on **SB** but **SB** had to withdraw all the criminal cases against his Younger Brother, who was arrested by police and kept him one night in the police custody in Kasba P.S. on non-bail able warrant due to his absconding report in the charge sheet against the first warrant submitted one year before and I.O. had to take action to avoid contempt of court for the non-execution of order. Moreover, it was announced that after three months again another meeting would be arranged calling the elder brother, $2^{nd}$ criminal, who was discharged in the first charge sheet but again a warrant was issued for the arrest on receipt of $2^{nd}$ charge sheet against order on Naraji Petition by **SB**.

When **SB's** water line connection had been cut and rolled with a plastic sheet, and on ........'2008 **SB** called a plumber to get it repaired that connection. Asstt. Secretary came and charged **SB** why he did not inform the authorities of Nagarik Committee and shouted on the plumber. However, **SB** replied he would put up this complaint in writing. After three days **SB** submitted the complaint along with the piece of pipe in the office of Nagarik Committee where new LCS, Abhisek, were present, and advised his secretary not to acknowledge any complaint in the record any more, which Mr. Nikhil had made a mistake by signing the first complaint one year before and

2nd time by his Secretary. Again **SB** wrote a letter addressed to Secretary, Nagaik Committee stating that he had withdrawn all the arrest warrants u/s.144(2) and u/s 107 and informed them that he was leaving Kolkata for bringing his family. After coming back in Kolkata, he again received one letter from the Secretary of Nagarik Committee that **SB** has to submit documentary evidence in support of the withdrawal of cases.

In ………. ' 2008, **SB** did produce the documents and a note in Bengali for Mr. Sudhir/Abhisek from General Secretary of …….. party of South 24 Parganas on the letter head of Nagarik Committee sent by Secretary. After that letter, **SB** was called for submission of his settlement note and plan of **'BRIDHYASHRAM'** as mentioned below. Below **SB** has given some details of correspondences between **SB** with Nagarik Committee and Police Station, Kasba.

## SUB: APPEAL TO NAGARIK COMMITTEE AGAINST THEIR ONE SIDED CONCLUSION TO SETTLE SB'S BROTHERS' DISPUTES

This is with reference to the 'conclusion' (sidhanta) of the memorandum of Nagarik Committee in respect of **SB's** brothers' disputes to be settled within three months announcing meetings and during this period both the brothers lived together in the above address and asked to maintain, peace and harmony. **SB** under severe constraint to seek their immediate solution by allowing to make renovation of all common uses of two brothers'available spaces and with separate gate as requested earlier received by Mr. Nikhil as per his official rank & position as Assistant Secretary including all supporting documents. Mr. Nikhil denied in the meeting as per notice and has read out **SB's** younger brother's complaint first, stating that this complaint received earlier than **SB's** complaint. A copy of the acknowledgement of complaint was attached for ready reference. There after Mr. Nikhil visited premises for checking on the receipt of younger brother's further complain for repairing of water line and immediately he charged **SB** that why **SB** had not informed before repairing the pipe.

Under the above circumstances **SB** thought that the officer of the Committee registered under law was an elected person who could interfere in every body's personal affairs entering in their premises any time as per his will and wish. If **SB's** thought was wrong, he would have never appealed to Nagarik Committee to restrict this person in the premises without **SB's** permission because this officer was supporting the criminals who already were convicted as per Police Report.

In view of the above, **SB** requested the Nagarik Committee to be kind enough to consider his appeal as local best judge going through **SB's** submitted documents before the scheduled date, otherwise series of various criminal cases filled U/Sec. 420, 406, 107 and 144 (5) might bring warrant against all. It is well known that the "Give and Take" policy could not be one sided. So long **SB** was giving to all as international donor, as **SB's** blood group is 'O' positive. In support of the above, **SB** submitted documents for their knowledge.

Finally, the above Nagarik Committee could not do anything and when **SB** informed that he is going to submit all the documents to Police Station for diary to appeal to Human Right Commission then LCS, **Abhisek** informed that the local young boys were supporting **SB's** younger brother and they might even attack **SB. SB's** earlier letter of dated....... to his Elder Brother, **Supriya"**

**My dear Dada,**

It is an eternal truth that our Existence in this Earth due to our Father and Mother's Love. You and our younger brother do not except the above truth when both of you are opposing me to build up one Memorial Trust in the name of our Father to fulfill our Father's last wish conveyed to me before leaving this Earth when I was in Gulf countries. As per his advice I wanted to build up **Old-Age-Home** on our joint property to be managed by our bove Registered **NGO–P. S. C. S.** and **Logo** of which also got **Trade Mark Registration Number.**

This **NGO** is non profitable organization with Cost Plus 10% for Reserved Fund. I am attaching **Old-Age-Home Brochure** for your kind reference.

I would like to remember some incidences of your extreme passion/Sex- hungry activities due to unsatisfactory marital-sex for which you were blaming our Father. Your passion increases when you find a woman/lady is busy in cooking in the kitchen and immediately you enter in the kitchen to show your skill in cooking and try to instigate and motivate the woman for your purpose. During my stay in Bombay you came once in my rented Flat and after some chit chatting you enter in the kitchen where my wife was busy in cooking. To make very close relation immediately you have changed your Zodiac Sign from Min Rashi to Kanya Rashi, because you were aware that my Wife's Zodiac sign is Kanya Rashi. There after you caught our younger Brother's Wife and neighbouring people also came to know from the sound of scuffle of my brother's wife with you. This matter you also confessed and explained to me with tears on your own when I came to your Flat. Then on ............ 2008 Justice D. K. B. did arrange Ist Counseling Meeting in his Office Room for settling our disputes of construction on our Joint Property of Land in the presence of all three Brothers. Just on starting time before justice's questionnaire our younger brother started telling that he will take care of our Elder Brother's defamation due to above incidence in our locality. I and Elder Brother never thought of such questionnaire will be arisen at all. This is happen out of confusion that taking advance money from the Elder Brother if my younger Brother forgets what to reply if any question arises from Justice D. K. B. Finally, Dear Dada have succeeded at the age of 73 through your extreme passion/ Sex-hungry you had to marry with your kitchen-mate, Smt. M. D. who was living in your Up-stair's flat which she got from her demised husband with one Black Colour Son. There after disposing off that Up-stair's Flat you have purchased new Flat opposite other side of L. Cinema, R. M. Colony, Dum Dum, Kolkata-. Now your extreme self motivated destructive Ego made confirm not to give me construction contract under my licensed Enterprise, S. B. C. S. recommended by you in the year 2004. And you are teaching our younger brother how to misbehave and torture me when he came to you to get your sanction for allowing me to construct the building on 50% Vs 50% ratio proposed by him and I agreed but he told that he will confirm after discussing with you. Since you have made him your slave by paying his required money and after few days when I enquired he loudly started telling that he does not have any relation with me whether a blood relation or any neighbouring relation and not supposed to give any reply and going inside his Room so many utterances for few minutes, which I have just listen silently without uttering a single word. Indirectly he is also tortured for carrying water whole day from one end to other end. I did offer him to install Toilet/Bathroom in his first Varanda so that I can make one new single Room on the same vacant place to bring my family permanently. How long you can keep your destructive Ego alive when you already got two attacks and you cannot carry with you if you are on aboard to hell or haven. By paying lump sum money to my advocate through your Advocate to file a defective petition without enclosures U/s 226 which will never appear in court as per our younger brother. For your portion you must have made some will for your beloved and now I am planning to file a recovery suit for Rs.............../- for construction against two brothers and Rs.............../- against business loan to younger brother up to and including 30.11.2014. For this I have written one letter to my advocate to take necessary action for my 5 cases. If I don't get any response I am going to file one cheating case U/s 420 for 4 people including my Publisher. I am attaching relevant copies of the above.

I am also attaching one letter addressed to Prime Minister of India enclosing therewith my 8th Edition of Book– **"Evolution of Human Beings and Society"** for your kind reference.

Now I am penning down with my Pranam to you. Yours middle Brother.

The concept of the above **BRIDHYASHRAM** initiated when **SB's** miseries started in his home when he has taken retirement from the services to get relief from huge debt for children's higher education and for booking of one flat for permanent shelter. **SB's** wife did not accept this voluntary retirement, considering that he would not be able to maintain the status quo, which he maintained throughout his working life and started misbehaving with him by taking control of their two children. Children's behaviour towards their father also changed at the same time and **SB** thought to commit suicide. He was wondering as to what for he sacrificed his own interests for making the children self-sufficient, by spending Rs............. for his son and Rs........... for his daughter for their higher education.

**SB** has intuition power by which he could foresee the ensuing debacles and his mind got disturbed and he took immediate step to prevent any debacles in near future. For instance, **SB** made one "family settlement deed" on stamp paper of Rs.100/- duly notarised after taking all four members' signatures. By this settlement deed he could claim Rs......... as maintenance charges for the whole life. And another one **"GENERAL POWER OF ATTORNEY"** from his wife for selling his new flat in........., 15 storied Millennium Tower, Maharastra for clearing a loan amount of Rs...... from HDFC Bank, Vashi Branch if monthly EMI of Rs...... paid by his son get stopped.

In the year 2006 when **SB's** son came on holiday from US, **SB** took his son's permission to meet him in his daughter's bank flat in Mumbai for the planning of settlement. Immediately after **SB's** entrance in his daughter's flat, his wife and son became furious and burst out by saying "**Mr. SB**" get out from this flat" and further threatened him with dire consequences and or else to call police for the purpose.

After coming back to Kolkata, **SB** suffered serious sickness, as he could not tolerate that sort of humiliation from his own children and wife. After few months, he decided to file divorce suit against his wife and recovery suit against his son. **SB** sent a notice through advocate to his son's office address and to his daughter's residence address. **SB** filed a divorce suit against his wife but he did not accept the exparte judgment because he loved his wife very much as against every body's dislike from his parent's side as well as her in-laws side.

Later on **SB** came to know that his brother in-law, Digbijoy had organized the marriage for both of his children and did not inform him and later he was refusing to give their settlement address. Such a cruel generation developed in the present society.

Further miseries started for mutation in Government's BLRO Office and thereafter in the Kolkata Corporation. In the year 2004, after registration part was over **SB** had taken help of his distant relatives, who was acting as agent for submission of BLRO mutation and Corporation mutation on payment of some advance. For BLRO mutation, SB has put up application during.......... first in combined one application and latter on separately three applications for three owners. In this office, one purposeful syndicate was formed unofficially for manipulation to extract extra money by making delays in all applications processing, starting from private group sitting outside BLRO Office for writing various application and selling judicial stamps to fix up in the application by charging high rate. Since **SB** was aware of application format, he did not seek any help from anybody and submitted his application after paying nominal extra amount for paying khajna for the land. Due to various reasons of delay from hearing, inspection, missing of files, complaining to BLRO **SB** got the mutation certificates in the month of ........'2005 after putting receipt signatures date of......'2007 as advised by the staff member.

Next **SB** did start Corporation mutation through the agent, **SB's** distant relative, who could manage Assessment Hearing Notice for tax valuation during ..........'2006.

When **SB's** agent informed that the expected estimate of about Rs.......... for 27 years tax arrears to be given, then **SB** had taken decision to be present on hearing day instead of Agent, to sit with hearing Officer for reducing the valuation explaining the status and position of the land. **SB** could convince hearing Officer to reduce the land valuation and accordingly could reduce almost 1/4th of the tax payment, which all agent demanded. Before this agent another agent demanded Rs............ of which first advance of Rs.......... and balance Rs.......... after assessment Bill. All the agents are having good relation with all the staff members of the Department for satisfying them with extra money by forceful pick pocketing from the Tax Payers. As per the private concern, there should be disposal report format, which every staff should submit every day to their respective bosses before they leave office duly signed. Moreover, this report format would be the parameter of their performance for further increment and promotion and should not judge by their service period. Register of applications, which is the first delay method for not taking application on the same day stating there are a lot of pending applications to enter in the Register and cannot give registration number for receipt of application in the same day and applicant, should leave application without any acknowledgement. Do you know why? Everybody knows the secret but nobody would come to tell you.

**Next come to Police Station:** - Police Force is considered as Rakhshak of all human beings and society. Nevertheless, in the present state of affairs, police insists on criminal offences to the complainant so that they can extract extra money from both the parties. **SB** submits here the various incidents of how he has become the worst victim even after satisfying the I.Os by paying extra money to get the relief from the criminals from their criminal offences: -

**SB** has filed a criminal suit U/s 420 and 406 against his two brothers for denying any amount accepted from **SB**

and allowed him to construct new building on the new land. Warrant had been issued to arrest both the brothers. The execution of this order assigned to I.O., BBB who was going to be retired very soon collected good amount of money from **SB** for giving charge sheet report giving reason that he had to pay 'Barababu' (Office-In-Charge). However, he had collected from both the brothers for submitting the charge sheet in their favour by reporting that the younger brother was absconding and elder brother got discharged giving reason that he did not fall under u/s 420 & 406.

On the receipt of **C**harge Sheet, court again issued non-bailable arrest warrant against younger brother during ………….. which was unexecuted till end of …….' 2008. After receipt of **SBs** S.O.S letter to the Officer-In-charge, directed I.O. to execute warrant.

On…….' 2008, night younger brother of **SB** was arrested and the next day morning got released by his advocate from the Court. Since then the family members took cruel attitude and have complained Nagarik Committee on which they immediately served notice for a meeting. Before this, in…………. **SB** did arrange u/s 144(2) court order for repairing and demarcation wall for both the lands for which **SB** had been advised by his Advocate some kharchapani, which paid to the I. O. Mr. Subir. But the said I.O. submitted report in favour of opponent parties because their amount of kharchapani was comparatively higher.

Next another Court Order u/s 144(2), arranged for repairing and demarcation wall, which assigned to another I.O. Mr. Asish who was promised by **SB's** advocate for high value of lump sum but advocate did not materialized the deal. **SB's** advocate smelled that the I.O. had collected huge amount from opponent parties and took transfer to another Police Station after submitting reverse Report than the agreed sample Report shown in advance that to mentioning wrong Case M.P. Number than the actual number so that nobody can trace out the Report of which counter signature done by Officer-In-Charge.

Due to cruel behavior of opponent parties, **SB** has filed F.I.R. in Police station and submitted a petition u/s 107. And for the above Petition court ordered for Report which same I.O. Mr. Asish submitted on the same day having no relevance of the subject matter even after submission of documentary evidence obtained from **SB's** Security personnel hired for short period for his safety and security.

Due to the above untoward happenings and finding no alternative **SB** had written a letter to the Honourable Chief Minister of West Bengal, Writer's Building, Kolkata for his kind intervention and settlement of disputes. The above letter had been acknowledged by the assistant secretary to the chief minister addressed to **SB** stating that he had been directed to acknowledge receipt of **SB's** letter addressed to the Chief Minister of West Bengal. The Asstt. Secretary to the Chief Minister to inform **SB** that the department of S. P., South 24 Parganas had been requested to consider the matter raised by **SB** and to take such action as is possible and to inform **SB** that the action was taken. Further correspondence in the matter, if necessary, might be addressed to the department". But, **SB** did not receive any letter from the department of S.P., South 24 Parganas. And another letter to The President of ......... Party, South 24 Parganas, West Bengal for attn: Shri Shyamlal who did not receive that letter with the enclosed Book with a comment: **"Your matter is a Hot Cake which you may give to proper Media and you can earn good money"**.

Next **SB** has written a letter to the Hon'ble Governor of West Bengal in the month of …….. for his help to depute a **NGO** to construct the proposed **Bridhyashram** after settling two brother's claim. OSD & E.O. Special Secretary to the Governor of West Bengal has forwarded the letter to the District Magistrate, South 24 Parganas, Alipore, Kolkata during March, 2009. On the receipt of the copy of the above letter, **SB** has written a letter to the District Magistrate and copy to the Secretary of Governor during ……., 2009. After a number of visits, DM has asked his OC, General, for report. OC had written a letter to SP, South 24 Parganas, West Bengal and 2nd reminder copy forwarded to **SB**. When **SB** sought an appointment with SP, South 24 Parganas during ……., 2009, S. P. said that the Police Department would act legally as per the Honourable Court's order and they would send status report to maintain the peace and harmony. They would not work under any circumstances on humanity consideration or social obligations. Then **SB** told to S. P. that the Police Department had liberty to earn kharchapani from both the parties (Complainant & Opposition) to prepare the status quo report in favour of who pays more money in terms of 'Kharchapani'.

**SB** being a senior citizen is facing lot of disturbances and sufferings through bank operational systems from Government Banking Enterprises and Private Banking Enterprises under control of Reserve Bank of India. Banking operational systems should be considered as emergency services and their Trade

Union right should be ceased under ordinance to prevent their strikes, work to rule, slogan, procession etc., which **SB** has already suggested in the previously mentioned chapter of Price Index. Because of their strike and work to rule right, bank customers do not get their own arranged pension through ECS from Postal MIS and from other sources for indefinite period. When their lending interest rate gets reduced and they get sanction from Reserve Bank to increase their various charges as compensatory relief, all banks have increased their charges two to three times more by their own discretion power. But all banks are taken advantage of this right and have started charging abruptly some times in wrong way also. When customer did challenge then they manipulate in accounting systems by passing journal vouchers and refund the charged amount. Some time if customer has issued some big amount of cheques from his CC A/c, in favour of one party having his A/c in the same bank in other branch and those cheques clearance have taken more than 7 days. Moreover, ATM withdrawal also made stopped because the CC A/c made deactivated for utilizing the money in market for short period on high rate. Likewise, some banks make purposely delay to give credit of transfer cheques to the customer CC A/c more than 4/5 days taking advantage of holydays and customer O.D. interest charged in addition rough behavior with that senior citizen customer. When customer put up complaints, Chief Manager does not want to acknowledge the complaint letter and keep the matters pending. Some banks directly paying their Card Division from their customer savings A/c without taking any concurrence from the account holder. Since **SB** being the victim of such transaction has filed a suit, and got the exparte judgment wherein order passed to pay the complainant his principal amount including legal expenses, interest and compensation totaling to Rs.......... approximately as against Rs............

**SB has written one last letter to his Elder Brother Supriya as mentioned below (Revised)**

# FINAL REQUEST TO ALLOW SB TO CONSTRUCT BUILDING ON HIS AREA AFTER SIGNING 'POWER OF ATTORNEY'AND/OR 'PARTITION DEED'

Ref: SB's earlier letter dated ........... 2015 sent by Speed Post and as per Postal Track Report Item delivery attempted but misspent, moved to Ballygunj, next to Ghugudanga-delivery attempted but addressee moved, next moved to Haltu for return to the Sender.

On ........... 2015 you have arranged one meeting at one rented house, Kayastha Para, Haltu where all together SB self, yourself and Younger Brother entered in that House and both of you agreed to award the contract to SB's **Self Enterprise-..................... Services'**, civil contractor for construction of Building on Joint Property of three Brothers @ 50/50 ratio (Owners' allocation at 50% and Builder's allocation at 50%) on the following terms and conditions:

As per final settlement and your advice SB had prepared draft of **'Power of Attorney'** as per agreed terms and conditions given by you consulting one senior most Advocate and submitted to you on ........ 2015, attaching one Letter on one **NGO Letter Head- "……… Society"** addressed to Joint Commissioner of Kolkata Municipal Corporation, Head Office including property Tax Bill of Rs…………/- approximately for three years for rebate considering construction of **Old-Age-Home.** If we accept this Bills (Original of which are retained by you) as it is then annual valuations of two lands showing Rs…………/- instead of Rs………./- and next GR-Rs…………/- instead of Rs………/- paid tax up to 2012 for 2 Cottahs 4 Chhittack and for 7.1/2 Cottahs of Land showing Rs………../- instead of Rs…….../- paid up to 2012. And all have to pay Property Tax Bill 6 times and 4 times higher than earlier Tax.

After one week when SB did not get any response from you about the **'Power of Attorney'** given to you for approval even after giving number of calls and SMS to your Mobile No. 9007709920 and when SB checked up to Younger Brother, while wishing Bijaya Dashami to him and his family who is residing in Front side of the Road in Two Rooms and Barandas attached with SB's Single Room with one Baranda confronted with the following questionnaires which bestowed on SB beyond his capacity and seems to be learned from you only.

The Younger Brother did ask about SB's credential and in reply SB told that he has arranged Builder, Architect, materials supplier and his own experience in construction line.

A) Then he argued about Architect's 50% mischievous calculation of Owners' portion and demanded your Architect to be deployed. SB's reply stand that can be challenged by any Architect of your choice.

B) Next he wanted to remove all of SB's attachment with all associations which was not cleared and assuming if it is for that linked **NGO**-"........................ **Society**" Non profitable organization about which SB explained earlier that this NGO is registered under West Bengal Society's Act and its 'Logo' also registered under Ministry of Registration, Government of India and obtained 80G Income Tax Exemption Certificate.

C) SB again given below detailed analysis including your whole life carrier and activities (Revised) which will be only reason of turning back to your commitment once committed. Quoted as it is from the letter by SB.

Our Younger Brother was telling that my age is now 73 years and I will be alive another 10 years and after that he will be able to construct the Building on his own. Poor Fellow does not know the span of our previous generation. Our Father's Elder Brother and Younger Brother, both demise before our Father and I can bequeath by Will of my portion.

D) i) I told my Younger Brother about you that being a Political leader generally back out from any commitment. They are power crazy destructive egoist. Your service life without any service because you were Eastern Railway's Union Leader who enter in office after 12 A.M. and ask office peon to bring Attendance Register from Bara Babu's table to your table and you sign then came out from office for selling Saris outside which witnessed by me when I came with you in your Howrah Statistical Department's Building. And this Union Leadership made your services suspended for few years by Railway Authority when you changed political party from

CPM to Naxalite and shifted to Chandan Nagar which was earlier a French Colony even after Independence.

ii) You were blaming father for your unsatisfied marriage due to deficiency in sexual impulse of your wife.

iii) Next you were giving stinging remark about my Job as apprentice @ Rs.150/- per month from my Company arranged by our Father and as per you it should have been given to you but you were already engaged in Eastern Railway @ Rs.150/- per month. My up-gradation started from Apprentice to Accounts Clerk, Asstt. Accountant, then Accountant, next Accounts Officer, Sr. Accounts Officer and then Next promotion ended as Manager (Accounts & Taxation) when I resigned from my services for coming back to Kolkata for improvement of Younger Brother's calamitous condition and recovery of our father's occupied 7.1/2 cottahs of land getting encroached by South and North side neighbours as per his continuous telephone calls with tears. Before leaving Kolkata in the year 1967 our Father took Oath from me saying that I should take total liability of our Younger Brother for life time because Father will not be able to give him proper education. Accordingly in the year 1969 when I got transferred from Assam to Rajasthan at Atomic Power Project and in Heavy Water Project I have arranged one job as Fitter Supervisor for our Younger Brother in the year 1970 after his completion of School Final up to Class Ten. Next in the year 1982 when my services got transferred in Gulf countries before that I did send back our Younger Brother to home for starting Business of Trading which arranged by our Father and for Trading Business I did remit to our Father Rs.5000/-. I had been receiving massage about his well to do position and got married. Next after coming back in India and in the year 1998 when I was on official Tour in Durgapur Steel Modernization Project for Auditing I could visit our Parental House to meet our Younger Brother and his family with two children who gave me a tremendous shock and pain looking their skeleton bones figure. I shouted on Brother and asked him why he did not contact me in our Bombay Head Office. Immediately I gave him one Bearer Cheque of Rs.10,000/- drawn on HDFC Bank of Bombay Branch. And going back to Bombay I did arrange one job for him in our Haldia Pipeline Project as Store and Purchase Assistant. And next after completion of Haldia Project I did arrange same job in our Bangalore Water Pipe Line Project. In the year 2003 when I resigned from my services our Brother could not continue. In our Company all projects staffs were respecting me and addressed me as 'Dada' as they were scared of my visit in Project Site for Auditing and they were taking care of my any request. All the above promotions shown in Sl.1F a(iii) achieved on my performance only. And in time to time due to my high profile performance Project Director of the Company used to change my designation as Billing Engineer in one Atomic Power Project, Rajasthan and as Project-In-Charge in Raigarh, Maharastra PIL Pipe Line Project.

Our Father was a great Pandit and Astrologer, Founder member of **Bishudhya Sidhyanta Panjika** before his demise. Whatever he has pronounced about me is 100% happened and at the last from his Old Aged pain due to neglected behavior from the own kith and kin he informed me in the year 1983 that I should be prepared for constructing **Bridhayshram** after entering in India and also told there will be no body to help me at my Old Age.

E) Another reason of your wrath on our Father due to your failure of avaricious attitude when In the year 1983 you did force our Father to give you Gift of 50% land from 4 Cottahs 4 Chhitak land which he did not agree then you made Sale Deed showing Receipt of Rs.4000/- from our Father without paying the said money and got registered 2 Cottahs of land on your name. There after sanctioning Plan by your Builder Mr Niranjan Saha you have constructed your building including encroachment of some part from our 2 Cottahs 4 chhitak land. This encroachment we got confirmation from KMC Engineer when given written reply for demolition of building on enquiry from the KMC Judicial Department based on my case against Mr. Prabir Kumar Chakraborty to whom you have sold the said Plot with constructed building and who did not agree to amalgamate both the attached land for further construction. While selling the Plot and building you did agree to pay compensation of Rs........../- to us for damaging our Land which gifted by our Father in my name and our Younger Brother's name to resist your further encroachment.

Sudden change in our Younger Brother's behavior towards me when he was receiving some stinging remark from his friends circle that his health and radish colour skin figure was developing due to my contribution after my arrival in Parental House. One day he was attacking me saying that why I am saying to his friends circle about my contribution. Factually I was not aware of anyone from his friends circle. Thereafter he started refusing to pay my monthly 3% commission on every purchase though he paid 3 purchase orders commission and thereafter he refused to pay anything. Main reason of refusal of my Commission and my Loan amount due to his loss in Business for taking Purchase Order on low quotation and supplying bad quality of materials and all parties stopped issuing any Purchase Orders and possibly not releasing his any outstanding dues amount also.

Next your refusal of allowing me to construct the Building on our Joint Property through my Own Enterprise- "…………………….. **Services**" registered under KMC Act recommended through your LBS, Mr. Saha. Your Political adamant attitude by helping our Younger Brother giving him money time to time due to which his arrogance bestowed upon me in such a manner as stated in Bengali saying- **(Aami aapnake kete tukro tukro kare mere felbo)** and as per your instructions and copying your characteristics incidences he started propagating various false incidences similar of your sexual passion diseases and others to all of my relatives, neighbours and friends' circle which I am facing from their changed behavior towards me and also being a guilty conscious he is refusing my offer to work with me in the construction period on monthly salary and repaying his business loan. Thereafter your Money Power being a Pensioner of Central Government started destroying all of my efforts for constructing Building on our Joint Properties shown as per details given below:-

First an Application u/s 156(3), Case No………../2007 dated …….. 2007 and recorded by Kasba P.S. Case No……. dated ……... 2007 u/s 420/406 – BGR-………/2007. Court has issued arrest Warrant Order for both of you but you could manage to get discharged from Kasba Police Station and for Younger Brother, Police Station sent absconding Report to Court. Next my Advocate put up Naraji Petition against you and you have been included in the same Petition. But Younger Brother's Arrest Warrant was in hanging and at the last fearing Contempt of Court Case against Officer-In-charge after one month S.I. at night at 11 O'clock arrested Younger Brother kept one night in the Police custody and that has become a bone of contention upon me which Younger Brother started circulating to all of my relatives, friends' circle stating that I have put him in Police Jail for one Night as per your advice. Ultimately after 5 years on your assurance that you will allow me to construct the Building on our Joint Property I have withdrawn this case unconditional on ....... 2012. But you have shown your Political destructive attitude denying and saying you will think later. Again as advised by one Advocate, S.D. attached with High Court and Supreme Court put up another Petition u/s 226 signed by his Sr. Advocate N.N.B submitted by the said Advocate, S.D.on ....... 2013 taking my signature without showing me the draft Petition which was one defective and will never appear in court for motion because that advocate was a professional cheating Advocate who contacted you and taken money from you extracting your money power. Otherwise the Case was sure to get final Order within a week as promised by him. Now here with this letter I am attaching a copy of **Brochure of Bridhyshram** by our non profitable **NGO- "............................…..… Society"** for your ready reference.

After studying the above history of your inhuman torture towards SB through younger Brother whom you have made your slave by giving him money time to time to torture SB for the last Nine years switching off SB's meter installed in his Room, keeping the common Tap open so that SB does not get water supply, not allowing SB to repair his Roof made of Asbestos Sheet and Fiber Sheet of Bed Room and Kitche with attached Bathroom, shifting the common Toilet/Bathroom in his two Varandas to allow SB to make additional Room to bring his family, ruffian behavior and your direct payment to SB's Advocates to manage Police Station not to execute the order passed by Judicial Magistrate under section 144(2) and other Acts to stop the above torture. Keep it in mind that the history of your inhuman torture towards SB have recorded in the Society being a Political Self-Centered Power Crazy Destructive Egoist left no stone unturned and not to keep SB to live in peace with sound health at this old age. And this history you cannot remove till your last day of your life in this earth but it will be framed in my Book- "**Evolution of Human Beings and Society" and "Indian Democracy**" which very shortly will be published around the World through one **Publishing Company in America.**

Now SB decided to forward this letter to the Central Government Pension Board and/or file a money recovery suit for both of you for construction and separately against Younger Brother for Business Loan if SB does not receive the **'Power of Attorney'** duly signed by both and/or **'Partition Deed' along with 'Chart'** attaching herewith within seven days from the date of receipt of this letter.

**Another incidence of one qualified advocate, Mr. Shiv Sankar** who had given services earlier to **SB's** elder brother, **Supriyo,** and since beginning of........., 2005 the said Advocate did start giving services to **SB**. Since **SB** was not having any idea about the charges of advocate he used to pay as per demands of the said advocate. On receipt of threatening call from **SB's** elder brother, **Supriyo** to the advocate that how he can take service of his younger brother against him. In the mean time advocate has taken advances from **SB** for various services but did not deliver proper services and **SB** had to submit petition to Bar Council of West Bengal giving full details of excess payments mentioned below:

| SL.NO. | PARTICULARS | EXCESS PAID (RS.) |
|--------|-------------|-------------------|
| 1. | One letter addressed to Pinaki, advocate demanded Rs.400/- and paid as against Rs.100/- which he is charging to others Hence excess paid .... | 300.00 |
| 2. | Complaint letter to Commissioner against Pinaki for illegal construction paid cash Rs.200+600 as against Rs.200/- hence excess paid | 600.00 |
| 3. | Another letter to Commissioner paid Rs.400/- as against Rs.100/- hence excess paid | 300.00 |

4.   Another letter to Pinaki for                100.00
     apology letter paid Rs. 200/- by
     cash against Rs.100/-.

5.   2nd letter to Pinaki by cash              100.00
     Rs.200/- as against Rs.100/-

6.   One letter to Hearing Officer,            300.00
     KMC against Pinaki Paid by cash
     Rs.400/- as against Rs.100/-

7.   2nd letter to Hearing Officer again       300.00
     paid Rs.400/- as against Rs.100/

8.   Letter to Secretary, Haltu               100.00
     Ganatantric-O-Unayan Adhikar
     Rakhsha Committee paid
     Rs.200/- as against Rs.100/-

9.   Draft of Development Agreement            500.00
     & Power of attorney paid
     Rs.1000/- by cheque as against
     Rs.500/-

10.  Final Development Agreement               300.00
     paid Rs.500/-by cheque as against
     Rs.200/-

11.  Notice to Son paid Rs. 500/-by            300.00
     cheque as against Rs.200/-

12.  Demanded Mobile for Advocate's           1800.00
     wife's name from Reliance paid by
     Credit Card with out any service

13.  Draft for Divorce Suit paid               300.00
     Rs.500/-by cheque as against
     Rs.200/-

| 14. | Notice to two brothers paid Rs. 800/-by cash as against Rs.400/- | 400.00 |
| 15. | Demanded advance Rs. 5000/- paid by cheque from O.D. A/c for filling suit against two brothers but could not prepare a final draft due to receipt of threatening call from elder brother being advocate's first client | 5000.00 |
| | **Total Excess paid** | **11 000.00** |

During ........., 2006 advocate explained his difficulty to type out any letter, petition etc. in type writer and finally demanded my spared PC including my services for teaching him computer to get relief from boring type writer. **SB** used to come every day morning and some time also in the evening at his residence for teaching how to operate computer and printer. Some times **SB** used to help him by typing some petition, letters, etc. when he gives dictation for typing in computer. During March 2007 **SB** went to Bombay and the said advocate used to call his assistant to operate P.C. result of which, Hard Disc of P.C. got damaged and **SB** has to purchase new Hard Disc. By Credit Card worth of Rs. 2300/-. Now total cost of Hard Disc, rental charges of P.C. & services work out to be Rs.11000/ and finally this advocate has to pay back Rs.22,000/- to **SB.**

This advocate was working in a private company and after losing job, he has obtained License for advocating job of writing letter, petition, but for filling petition he transfers the case to other leading advocates for attending and hearing dates and next further proceedings in the court.

This advocate is using one Jewellery Shop in Gariahat as his office for caching client and his agency business for the Jewellary Shop. And by cheating method this advocate is also trying to recommend house hunting people to invest money in Particular Real Estate Company so that he can manage one permanent job in this company.

Another quality of this advocate when he finds some clients are disturbing he frequently for filling a petition for which he has taken advance money then he deputes is wife to insult those clients for getting out from his residence and on that particular day he pretends as bed ridden sick person.

**The said Advocate filed a Counter Criminal Case U/s 500 against the above complaiant to the learned Chief Judicial Magistrate, Alipore, Kolkata Police Court.**

**As disputed titled 'Accused' Opponent Party filed a Petition for dismissal of the above Case as mentioned below:-**

District: South 24 Parganas
In the Court of Learned Chief Judicial
Majistrate, 9th Court, Alipore.

**<u>AC-Case No.P-........../14</u>**
**In the Matter of:-**

**Petition under Section 181/191/500 I.P.C.**

In the Matter of:

Shri Shiv Sankar, Son of B. Chakraborty, by profession – practising advocate, residing at Thakur Bari Road, P. S. Tallygunge, Kolkata–700026, District 24 Parganas (South)..................... **Complainant**

And

Sri SB..............................., Son of Late .............., residing at .........................., P.S. Garfa Kolkata – 700078 .....………. **Accused**

## Petition for dismissal of the Case

The humble Petition on behalf of the disputed titled **'Accused' Opponent Party**

Most Respectfully Sheweth:-

1. That the disputed titled **'Accused'** name given by the Complainant is peace loving and law abiding citizen of India and the Author of Books of '..........................................' and '.........................'.

2. That the Opponent Party is a Founder Secretary of one **NGO- "…………….....................… Society"** registered under West Bengal Societies Act for **Old-Age-Home** which has also obtained its **Logo** Registration Number from the Ministry of Indian Trade Mark Registration and also obtained **80G**

**I.T. Exemption Certificate**, Copy of **Letter Head** attached, marked as **Annexure- A/1**.

3. That the Opponent Party did also register his own Self Enterprise–**S.B. ...........................** as Civil Contractor for constructing **Old-Age-Home,** copy of **Letter Head** attached marked as **Annexure-A/2** on his land which could not be materialized because of obstruction raised by his two brothers against whom the Opponent Party wanted to file a suit and paid Rs.5000/- advance to the above **Complainant, Sri Shiv Sankar** who could not prepare the Petition on receipt of the Opponent Party's Elder Brother's threatening call as political Leader. This indisplined matter was also included in the Petition against the above **Complainant** in Bar Council, Kolkata.

4. That the Complainant in his Petition Sl. No. 1 & 2 given his Professional credential that he is practicing as Advocate for more than 37 years in good faith and due care with honesty and sincerity for numerous cases in all most all Courts, self and/or as an assistant for attending with the Senior Advocates. But the Complainant having same age of the Opponent Party forgot to mention his service period in some organization in legal department which he told to the Opponent Party when both were very close friend disclosing all personal matter to each other's past history of their life. One of his Self-Confession Statement which includes the above history attached with the Petition in Bar Council, a copy attached and marked as **Annexure-A/3** which he is now stating as concocted statement in his present Petition Sl. No.3.

5. That the Opponent Party would like to put up some incidences happened before filling his Petition to the Bar Council that one day the Opponent Party saw his friend, the present Complainant was sitting in the Resident Chamber of one Senior Paneled Advocate from Justice D. K. Basu & Co., Advocate S. S. Mukherjea who was also in a position of Judge for some period (learned from reliable sources), residing in Behala. In his residential Chamber The Opponent Party had been directed by Justice D. Basu for drafting one petition against one Cheater, ................ dvising to carry Cash of Rs.2000/- but the said Advocate very honestly taken a cheque of Rs.800/- only for draft petition which was not up to my satisfaction. Before filling the Complaint Petition to Bar Council against Sri Shiv Sankar the present Opponent Party shown his Petition to Adv. S. S. Mukherjea who advised the Opponent Party not to submit any complaint against the Adv. Shiv Sankar stating that he is their advocates' Cast and he is coming to him for showing his petition for checking and editing purpose.

6. That other various incidences are mentioned in the Self-Concession Statement of the Complainant mostly witnessed by the Opponent Party sitting in the Room of Complainant's New Flat.

7. That after last hearing and submission of all documents showing Originals Bills and Receipts the Opponent Party was sure that he will get the Order in his fever after 5 Years. But when he received the Order on .............. 2014 he got shock and consoles himself that remembering Adv. S.S. Mukherjea's

statement that nobody can challenge any advocate from advocates' Cast. It is obviously one telephone call which can dismiss any case in favour of Advocate, evidently the Order date was on .......... 2014 but Order passed on ......... 2014.

8. That another incidence of receiving one E-mail dated .................. 2014 addressed to the Opponent Party's E-mail No. from one Junior Advocate S. Sarkar of One Self- styled Senior Advocate S. Datta who directed Mr S. Sarkar to send one draft letter for the Opponent Party's E-mail address to the President, Disciplinary Committee, Bar Council of West Bengal, .................... Road, Kolkata-700001for Case No......... 2008 in the Matter of Opponent Party Shiv Sankar. Re: Application for praying for adjournment the above mentioned case matter for about 6 weeks from Today, the ........... 2014 cause, suffering from high fever and other diseases. Whereas Order has been passed on ........... 2014, A copy attached and marked as **Annexure-A/4.** This Adv. S. Datta is another commission earning Advocate like my friend, Adv. Shiv Sankar When the Opponent Party approached this commission earning Advocate, S. Datta as per his advice for filling in National Bar Council, Delhi challenging the Final Order of Kolkata Bar Council dated ........... 2014 he immediately turned back when I reached New Delhi stating that this is Santida's Case hence he cannot do it. The Opponent Party got relief from his statement for saving the demand of huge amount by this Advocate.

9. That the Opponent Party is attaching one letter for your kind perusal marked as **Annexure A/5** addressed to Mr. Shiv

Datta 6 pages narrating massacre of 5 cases by taking cash money from the opposite party and submitting incomplete Petition in the appropriate Court so that the Petition will not move for hearing or will be dismissed on first hearing and/or compelled the party to withdraw the case.

10. That Referring Sl. No.4 & 5 the Complainant wanted to proof the Opponent Party's usual insanity due to which the Complainant is taking as the Opponent Party is contriving and intending to injure the Complainant in his profession after a long gap from the date of Final order passed on 10.02.2014. The Opponent Party feels some third party is instigating the Complainant to awake up and hammer the worst victim further, the **disputed titled Accused** who has entered in his parental House after 40 years and landed first in the Court of Law under control of **20% Burgeon People over 80% APL & BPL Categories** of People in the present Democratic Society ruling with Autocracy.

However, at the present capacity and financial crisis the Opponent Party can beg for apology forgetting all of his losses and due to his insanity as the Opponent Party think did make any harm at all to him. Also pray for dismiss the Case and release his Bond money of Rs.500/-.

**There is another incidence of conducting tour programm** with 7 family members of one club of yoga and laughter therapy by giving challenge for completing two packages Tour in Southern Zone by 1/3$^{rd}$ price of Rs.6500/- per head as against the Rate of Rs.19000/- per head of Regd. Travel Agents' Rate. But **SB** had to face lot of mental tortures and threats for not refunding their immoral claim raised by representatives of those 7 members and loss of his own spending money of Rs.8000/-. Finally the club executive members arranged a meeting to safe guard the complain of one senior citizen aged 75 years old having support of well established member of present party king in Garfa area passed the following Exparte Judgement Order to make all the 7 members happy.

## EXPARTE JUDGEMENT ORDER ................

Order passed on ............. by the Jurists, all club members, expert in judicial matters decided by the secretary of the said club for laughter yoga centre in the presence of following members:-

**A.**  1.  Shri.X.B., Club Member as Jurist,
    2.  Shri D.K.C., Secretary.
    3.  Shri S.C., President.
    4.  Shri B.C.R. Vice President,

**Herein after referred to as the "Jurists members"**

**B.**  1.  Shri B.D.,
    2.  Shri G.P.D.,
    3.  Shri S.C.D.,

All club members and representatives of 7 Tourists members

**Herein after referred to as the "Complainant"**

**C. against S.B.**, Joint Secretary of the club, undertaken Packaged Tour as an unauthorized Travel Agent, herein after referred to as the "**Opponent, Other Party**".

## Following Order passed

Against **SB. Joint Secretary** of the above mentioned Club, who conducted Tour Programme of (Two packages) together as unauthorized Travel Agent to establish the challenged rate **@ 1/3$^{rd}$ rate of Rs.6500/- (Cost Plus10%)** per head without Entry Fee & Guide fee as against the Authorised Registered Travel agent. This authorized Agent's rate is Rs.19, 000/- per head approximately for two packages in Southern Zone. One of the Club Member, Smt. Bharati Roy who went on tour with M/s K. Special during October 2009 has confirmed that for one package tour she had to spend Rs.10, 000/- per head.

## Following Refund Order Passed:-

| | | |
|---|---|---|
| 1. | Total cost @ Rs.6500/- for 7 Tourists worked out to be | = Rs. 45,500.00 |
| 2. | Total payment received from 7 Tourists | =Rs. 37, 570.00 |
| 3. | Add: payments made by 7 Tourists for expenses incurred directly w.e.f. to | = Rs. 4, 500.00 |
| 4. | Less: Entry Fee, Guide charges & coolly charges paid by S.B. | = Rs. (2190.00) |

5. Add - Rs. 8,000/- paid by S.B. by mistake shown as paid by 7 Tourists on belief from the oral statement of Shri B. G. D. aged 75 years Senior Citizen in one statement which on looking to the said statement Shri G.P. D was under so much illusion that he asked S.B.

The said amount is paid by them correct? And having doubt after bank reconciliation later on corrected by SB is a criminal offences as per Jurists verdict. Hence to b e added back Rs.8000/- and Total Payments and Receipts made (2 to 5 & 1) =-47880.00+45500.00

6. Balance to be refunded (1-2 to 5) to 7 Tourist = Rs.2380.00

7. To satisfy the 7 Tourists' demand for refund of further Rs.15,000/-, Jurist finally decided after doing cost analysis and ordered to penalise S.B., unauthorized Travel Agent further Rs. 9,500/- to be refunded to 7 Tourists within six months.

To be signed by the Jurists Body.........................

What a beautiful contradictory Judgment- 1. one side lump sum rate of Rs. 6,500/- per head accepted for the complete two packages tour and other side jurists are making cost analysis to give refund to the 7 Tourists for their satisfaction. And **S.B.**, having no support from club members has to give away the following amount spending from his pocket for completing the two packages tour @ Rs. 2,367/- per head for two packages including further penalty of Rs. 9,500/- details of which are given below :-

1. By mistake amount shown as receipt from 7 Tourists=Rs. 8000/-

2. Further Cash withdrawn from ATM & spent for tour expenses could not accommodate in the statement = Rs. 8000/-

3. Further penalty if paid after cost analysis

**Total extra contribution to be made by S.B.=Rs. 25500/-**

Hence actual payment received Rs.37570/- plus direct spending Rs.4500/- will be reduced to Rs.16570/- after reduction of Rs.25500/-as against total package amount of Rs.45500/-. And with a request to Shri G..P.D. to confirm that he did agree to increase the rate of two packages tour @ Rs.7000/- per head totaling to Rs. 49000/- for 7 Tourists after landing in Secundrabud. **By this S.B. got the lesson in this society, if we want to give relief to any one by honest way we would land in trouble and miseries.**

**SB again has landed in financial trouble for helping one needy person for his trading business, who later on has established as a great cheater and has prepared his confession statement as mentioned below:-**

## SELF CONFESSION OF ONE CHEATER

I, Sri Cheaterlal, owner of m/s Trading Company hereby confess that on............ I gave call to Sri **SB** whom I knew from Chitta Ranjan Park Kali Bari, where, both were staying in room NO.... dormitory and both became very closed relation as uncle and nephew. on the basis of good understanding and having same zodiac sign as **'Aries'** after coming back in

Kolkata, Bhadreswar I took a chance and gave him a call to remit Rs............. to my UBI Current A/c No............. when I have only nominal cash for daily expenses and bank balance of Rs...... with ........... I., Bhadreswar Branch. I was under tremendous pressure and tension to clear my long outstanding loan of Rs............. which I did not disclose to Sri **S.B.** while signing notarized agreement on......, 2009 for showing working capital of Rs............ inclusive of Rs........... which was paid to S/debtors after date of.......... for arriving 60% profit for my self. actual working capital should be Rs.......... i.e. Rs....... minus Rs......... outstanding of S/creditors not shown in the agreement but on receipt of Ist remittance of Rs............ on............ promised to pay **Sri SB** as compensation @ Rs.30000/-p.m. on Rs.1,00,000/- considering 100% profit. later on changed to Rs.25,000/- p.m. again I requested for further two lakh Rupees but **Sri SB** insisted for the Agreement to be notarized at Shrirampur, Hooghly which has been done on ......... 2009. While drafting the Agreement I have changed the payment terms as 40% profit to **Sri S**B and 60% for me instead of Rs.25000/- P.M per one lac to **Sri S.B.** shown in Agreement then I have to change the Agreement when profit sharing system to be considered **Sri SB** as my partner and accordingly following terms and conditions have been agreed.

**1.** The borrower has agreed to receive the said advance amount from the lender for his trading business of agricultural products and other miscellaneous products as per consignment value basis on condition that the repayment of the loan received from the lender to be repaid @ 25% per month on 30th of every month. Plus O.D. interest for the utilized amount after the realisation of invoice value of the sold consignment against which the loan given, to be deposited in lender's Bank OD A/c no.…... with SBI,…. branch, Kolkata and another OD A/c No.……. with UBI, ……, Kolkata and due compensation @ 40/60 ratio on profit to be paid immediately after completion of accounting of two months business turnover.

**2.** If the repayment of the loan exceeds more than 15 days then the loss and damages caused due to delay, the borrower has to pay additional compensation @10% over the normal agreed 40% profit sharing ratio.

**3.** Lender has also agreed to provide all services in person or deputing his own assistant along with his office appliances such as Laptop, Computer, Printer, stationeries etc. for preparation of purchase bill, sales bill, consignment note etc. and delivery of the same to the customer, and collection of payments. Lender has also agreed to give all assistances like business partner to the borrower for procurement of agricultural products and other miscellaneous products jointly or singly by involving himself in entire business transactions. The borrower should provide an advance payment for all expenses to be incurred by the Lander.

**4.** In the last page of the agreement both parties have signed the oath and affidavit stating that we will not hide anything while dealing in the business and/or will not make any false excuses for delaying the repayment of bank loan to avoid tension between the parties. After registration of the agreement, **Sri SB** had withdrawn from his SBI OD A/c for Rs…….. And deposited Rs……… to my UBI A/c then Rs………. retained with him in his UBI OD.A/c to deposit to my UBI A/c for procurement of materials on time to time on or before date……… as per my requirement. First compensation of Rs.2200/- instead of Rs.25000/- paid to **Sri SB** during …….., 2009 by part by part. during……, 2010 I was planning for ginger trading, collecting from Assam for selling to Delhi, Kolkata, Siligury and other places around 50 trucks load, for which I require at least Rs.600000/-. As per Agreement, Working Capital of Sri **SB** shown as Rs…….... as per his all OD A/cs with SBI, UBI, & Axis Banks and accordingly I requested Sri **SB** to release further loan of Rs.3, 00, 000/-. Then **SB** agreed to arrange from his Axis bank OD.A/c for which I have open one current a/c with Axis Bank in Chandan Nagar Branch on…....... 2010. As per my requirement I requested for Rs.50,000/- on…....... 2010 which I received. and 0n….. 2010 I have received four cheques forRs.75,000/- each of two cheques and Rs.50,000/- each of two cheques deposited in my Axis Bank A/c and got cleared on…... 2010. Totaling Rs.3, 00, 000/-. Grand Total Rs.6, 00,000/-. Since I was penniless to start my business because of my brother-in-law's cancer treatment, who then expired. After receipt of this money I could regain my business strength but again my sister's cancer treatment was disturbing my business concentration, which I could not bear and finally discussing with doctor we did start giving her high dose of sleeping pills when she used to suffer unbearable head ache. Before starting this treatment, all of our home members arranged transfer her husband's property, where we were living, in our name taking her signatures on the documents. one day we have increased number of pills by which she fell on comma and 3$^{rd}$ day, on ………'2010 she expired. That day I was terrifically under tension for delay of doctor's arrival for issuing death certificate after verification, which took more than one hour because doctor was also in tension for issuing such certificate. Somehow I got relieved after completion of funeral work in electric burning Chula. Now I feel like bird and with full concentration my business started flourishing in full swing and I am paying every month rs.25,000/- to **Sri SB** part by part. My luck started favouring me in all respect after getting new business i.e. one stone field in Rajasthan belonging to father of Sri Gulmohar. I have been invited to visit the site of that stone field. Initially while visiting their stone field I have collected some stones weighing 19 kg which after cutting 4 kg specious stones (Jewells) have received after paying Rs.45000/- to Mr. Majender Bahel for his cutting charges. All those stones I have disposed off in jaipur, which I did not disclose correctly to my partner, Sri **SB** till date with bad intention. Next when Gulmohar and family making a lease agreement for 99 years of stone field of 10, 000 sq.ft. Between Shivlal, landowner and I, Sri Cheaterlal as execution activator for collecting stones. and another agreement between 4 partners namely Gulmohar, I.K. chohan, R.R. Chohan, Son of J. K. Chohan, Ram Bihari, stone cutter and I, Cheaterlal for investment and execution. I have already invested for the followings:-

1. Registration Rs.90,000/-
2. Labour charges - Rs.80000/-,
3. Tube Well & other infrastructure -Rrs.75000/-

From the sources of income from old stone sold money. when lease Agreement draft and registration taking time, I have collected further huge stones and dispatched by two car dumping in the back side of the car to Sri Majender Bahel for cutting and making Jewells. I paid further Rs.1,10,000/- to Ram Bihari during April'10. I did inform Sri **SB** that if Gulmohar and party failed to make proper agreement for giving me lease of that land for 99 years on my name for my security then I am going to dispose those collected stones. And I will be able to earn one core rupees from which I did promise to pay Sri **SB** over telephone Rs.25,00,000/- and for confirmation I have igned file note on…....... However, as per Mineral's' Act government should get 26% royalty. I am making delay to dispose of those Jewells out of cutting stones for high rate at common wealth game during October '10 when rate will be high on arrival of foreigners. At present I have kept all the Jewells under my custody.. Now I am refusing to give stock value to **Sri SB** saying I do not want to take risk of disclosing the present Jewells' value due to fear that may reach to Sri Gulmohar.

Now I am diverting this matter to one another new deals to **Sri SB,** i.e. taking one tea estate near Darjeeling by arranging foreign fund worth of one hundred crores of rupees from one international don and party. For this new deal, new company has been registered in Delhi by name M/s Devanan Tea Estate Private Ltd. with the following members namely:- K.P, Aggarwal, Dipak ggarwal and Cheaterlal. New Bank A/c with Oriental Bank Ltd. for entering into all these by depositing Rs.50000/- by me on ……. 2010 and by others for entering into all these new assignments. I have arranged to make one reserve fund depositing huge money in M/s Bank of India, Rishi Bankim Avenue, Bhadreswar A/c No......... This deposit money includes total collection of money from Jewell's sold in jaipur, and from ginger trade during ........ 2010 to............. 2010 and disposal value of my wife's parent's land, 1 Bigha 8 Chhatak near Hooghly railway station. And further I manage to make one sale deed of another plot, 3 Bighas, near Hooghly Station belongs to my wife's parent's land, which I have shown to Gulmohar's representative who visited and witnessed that land, and taken a copy of sale deed by that representative. During this period I was running again short of fund for my day to day expenses while staying in Delhi. For all the new deals I have again started putting pressure on **Sri SB** for further fund. I have again started taking from Mr. Kalam Das, whom I treat as son of a Beach (dog) and this I have told to **Sri SB also,** when he was started enquiring about my movement and telling that he is not getting his huge due amounts from me. Practically I could manage any time any place just giving few hours in any Mondi by purchasing and selling agricultural products, but due to fear from Sri Gulmohar I could not do so, reason I have promised that I will close my M**/s Trading Company** and will never remain busy in such trading job. Accordingly I did inform **Sri SB** that I am going to hand over the trading business to my brother and **SB** to cover my total outstanding dues of about Rs.60,00, 000/- to **Sri SB. A**fter finalization of accounting without stock which I am not willing to do and avoiding to meet him by telling lie every day and twisting him by giving various fictitious news about my progress from which he will also become Crore Pati. This has been conveyed through Dr.

Marric Dirchi, who is also one of the party in our various deals and I also confirmed to **Sri SB** that I want him as my mediator since I am academically very poor to communicate anything in English to others and foreigners. So long, I have been waiting for their arrival in our Common Wealth Games during first week of august'10. However, under pressure I have signed statement of accounts up to........... 2010 on........... earlier when I took fund of Rs.3,00,000/- I have committed that I am going to supply fifty 50 Trucks of gingers which will give us net income of Rs.13,00,000/- out of which **SB** will get 50% share about Rs.6,00,000/- and including this **Sri SB** will get total of Rs.18,00,000/- excluding Rs.25,00,000/- out of Rs. One Crore shown as stock in hand on....., 2010 and has been signed on....., 2010 statement including trial balance and confirmed vide file note signed by me on ........ 2010 for disposing of Jewells out of stone collected from Gulmohar's stone field in Rajasthan after common wealth game period. Today on...... 2010 early morning **Sri SB** arrived in my room for urgent need of Rs.3,00,000/- for which I issued one post dated cheque of dated ...... 2010 from my savings account no........ I cannot deny that all of my business growth and all these new business deals happened only because of contributions /investments received from **Sri S**B right from October' 2009 and continued till now by which I have regained my strength and could manage to long pending marriage on...... 2010 without informing anybody including **Sri SB.** However, **Sri SB** did know all these matters from my family members. After marriage, I have become owner of one new flat in Chandan Nagar & various lands. But I have given all false addresses to **Sri SB** so that he cannot find out about my new ownership. (CHEATERLAL)

# LETTERS TO ALL CONCERNED OFFICERS ON THE SUBJECT MATTER

**SB** decided to put up the above matter to the Central Bureau of Investigation, New Delhi to the following address:

**Superintendant of Police, Central bureau of Investigation, Anti Corruption Branch, New Delhi, Ist Floor, Block No.4, C.G..O. Complex, Lodhi Road, New Delhi - 110003**

**Sir,**

**Sub: Huge Cash Transactions in the year**

## 2011 Through Mr. Cheaterlal,

I, the undersigned, Sri S. C. Bhatt, business partner of Mr.Cheaterlal hereby submit some facts and figures in support of the following documents and there after latest conversations and incidences since January'11.

1. Latest Self Confession statements of Mr. Cheaterlal signed on....... when he issued one post dated cheque of Rs.... for dated ......... drawn on UBI, New Delhi, from his A/c No......... which has been deposited on .......... and due to insufficient fund the cheque has come back for insufficient fund with note from Bank on............ And also a copy of translated in Bengali of his Self Confession statements dated .......... which has been

sent by Registered post with A/D on .......... to his mother & to him jointly with attaching the followings:

2. Trial Balance and Accounts Statements up to and including .......... along with one File Note signed on........... for income of Rs...... for sale of precious stones out of which Rs....... to be given to Sri S. C. Bhatt after sale of precious stones during Common Wealth Game. Detailed statement given in Self Confession statement mentioned above.

3. A list of Fixed Assets worth of Rs..... statement signed by him.

4. Copy of Partnership Agreement notarized on........... during 2011, Mr. Cheaterlal informed Sri **SB** that he is going to get Three and half Crores rupees and there after Rupees Five Crores through Hundi In Barabazar area. After distribution to all parties, he was going to clear my outstanding from his share. On ............. at 11.40 Night through his Mobile No..........., now changed through portability to Voda phone as informed, that he is going to receive the entire cash on .......... and called me to wait in Howrah Bus terminus at 2.00 Pm on ............ for handing over some cash against my outstanding. But I was waiting till night up to 9.00 PM and again he gave call at my residence at the same night 11.00 Pm confirming that he is going to come to my residence next day 102102on .......... at 2.00 Pm to 2.30 Pm to clear my dues. Another bluff, and ultimately he switched off his mobile. During ............. '11 onward, he started cooking up new story that he is going to get his share from the Delhi Party after clearing

some documentary evidences, which took more than one month. Ultimately, from his various cooked up statement his entire group is under Net of CBI cell in 2G Scam case. The undersigned being a business partner of Mr. Cheaterlal wanted to catch hold of him for collecting various new agreements with M/s Gulmohar's family members whose residential address is at ............ Delhi, Contact No. ............. and with other parties mentioned in his confession statements. On............. I along with some of my friends have raided his house but he was absconding and he never turned up in his residence due to his mother's warning till he clears my outstanding. Time to time he used to inform me his development that he was staying with his fiancée in Hooghly and later on got married mentioned in his confession statements, possibly another bluff and again he has informed that he has done his new house entry ceremony where he will invite me on some day. From his statement I have come to know that some family members brother/sister of Mr. Gulmohar are working in some ministerial departments namely Miss Mira Kumar who was also staying in the same address of Gulmohar's family, i.e...........New Delhi but presently shifted to some Government Quarter in Lodi Road area. Since Mr. Cheaterlal was also under CBI net, his all bank accounts, Pan Card etc have been ceased. Accordingly, Mr. Cheaterlal collected all of my bank accounts with UBI, SBI and with Axis bank where his Delhi Party will remit directly in my accounts. I understood it is another bluff when I asked for E-Mail message confirming date and value of each remittance and could not send. From............, 2011 onward he confirmed on............... 2011 that he has submitted all his papers and CBI Officer has given him a copy of clean certificate, after CBI got clearance from Home Ministry, of which one copy to him and others to his counter party and to the respective banks by direct mail. Then he again twisted the earlier statements that now all remittance will be transferred to his accounts and he will be allowed to remit from his accounts to my accounts by date......... Since....... 2011 onward his mobile was switched off till ...... 2011 and on...... 2011morning at........ AM he rang me on his mobile and informed me due to Ram Navami in Rajasthan all Banks are closed and remittance cannot be made. On ........ morning he again rang up and could not make transfer due to non receipt of CBI clean certificate in his accounts and confirmation of money transfer in his accounts with UBI and in Axis Bank. Mr. Cheaterlal has further informed that he will be for one month in Rajasthan. Again he rang up at........ night on ........ and confirmed that he has put 3 post dated cheques of Rs...... each in his A/cs with UBI, deposited in Rajasthan Branch for transfer on my 3 A/cs with UBI, for value date on........ Out of my 3 A/cs, one is fully utilized O.D.A/c of Rs......, one S.B. A/c balance of Rs...... and one my company A/c of balance Rs...... Next on......... will go to Axis Bank to check his A/Cs status. Further payment he will make from Axis Bank A/Cs for value date on.......... Then he will check his Delhi parties for remittance after they receive CBI clearance certificate.

Now I understood why they have taken all of my A/Cs with UBI, SBI, Axis Bank, which is mostly O.D. A/Cs and Savings A/Cs with very low balance for purpose of ceasing because I have threatened Mr. Cheaterlal I will put the case to CBI. Mr. Cheaterlal academically very poor but he understands English matter after listening from some one's reading and he will ask to change for corrections wherever he wants. His confessions statements also he has changed several times through me lastly, he signed on......... He has also given me his authority letter of all A/Cs with UBI, Axis Bank and Bank of India for taking out statements for accounting purpose. Bank of India did refuse to give statement of accounts because there is a Pass Book, which shows only Rs........ when he did open a savings Account. He never updated the Pass Book as he has told that the entire business income he has deposited in that account as security deposit for those business deal with M/s Gulmohar and parties. But,........ on word there is no contact any more till date.

Yours truly,<br>
Encl: as above

Same subject matter has been written to the DIG, CID, Government of West Bengal, Bhawani Bhavan, Alipore, Kolkata- 700027.

## Another incidence of same type Advocate, S.D. details of whom are given below:
## **<u>FINAL REQUEST REVISED LETTER</u>**

Sri S. D., Advocate,
Supreme Court of India, Bar Liabrary, Room No.1
High Court, Calcutta, Bar Association, Room No.4

Sir,

On ........... 2014 after filling petition No....... of 2014 against Pannalal Roy in National Consumers Disputes Redressal Forum with reference of rejected orders of our Petition against Pannalal Roy in State Consumers Disputes Redressal Forum. I forgot to collect my Pen Drive from the Typist who typed Petition in his computer and copied in my Pen Drive after taking Print out near Advocates' Office, Supreme Court, New Delhi. By mistake I requested you when you were scheduled to catch hold the train on....... 2014 to bring that Pen Drive and hand over the same to the undersigned but you did not respond a single call since morning on ............ 2014, details of which are given below:-

| | | | |
|---|---|---|---|
| 1. | 28.07.14 | - Mob. No. 9163 061567 | - 7.35 AM No respond. |
| 2. | - do - | - Mob. No. 9831347488 | - 7.39 AM No respond. |
| 3. | - do - | - Mob. No.- | -do -9.25 SMS sent for Pen Drive |

4.  - d0      - Mob.-      No...... 13.37 PM, talked to Didi, your wife who advised to meet you in High Court.

5.  - do -    - do -       14.25 PM, Again talked to Didi who complained that I paying your Fees after getting the job done but I confirmed that all payments are made 100% in advance to you before doing the job

6.  - d0 -    - Mob No....  14.34 PM- Gave a missed call & no respond

7.  - do -    - Mob No.-    do - 14.35 PM -Suddenly you shouted upon mesaying why I have complained to your wife for Pen Drive

8.  - do -    - Mob No.-    could not note down In the Evening your commission Group Agent Mr. Sankar Mandal started shouting by saying that I should be be prepared for facing defamation case against me.

9.  - 2014 -  - Mob. No.-   8.49 AM- I have confirmed the receipt of Pen Drive from your Agent.

About you I have come to know from your Senior Advocate, **Sri N. N. B.** who arranged your sitting position in Supreme Court, Bar Library, Room No.1, as your communication address. You are arranging client and making all petitions by your Senior Advocates for your clients from whom you are collecting huge amount for your commission and Senior and Junior's Fees for petition and for attending on hearing days. You do not allow any complainant while filling the petition neither show him the draft petition because your tendency to keep the petition non admissible and not move from Monthly list to Day list for collecting further fees for resubmitting the petition to upper court or in Supreme Court keeping your Senior and Junior in confidence using the complainant as **Hallal Bakra.** On ........ 2014 while enquiring from Mr. N.N.B., your Senior Advocate about your absenteeism on admission hearing date he told that you are hiding from getting arrested for warrant issued for taking Rupees Three lakhs from Mr. ......... for Car.

Now I am constrained to notify the followings for your immediate action to give result/justice and Final Order as per your commitments. I am further landed in financial trouble due to nonpayment of my MIS of Rs........./- from Rose Valley on Deposit of Rs............/-. Mr. S.J., Publisher and your Group Agent, Mr. S. M. alarmed me and advised me to withdraw all of my deposits in Private Companies on 15% commission to the Committee established by MP, Sri ....... and other MPs/ MLAS as per all companies terms and conditions by which I will lose sufficient Principal Amount. And I have no capacity to file a suit at the moment.

I did send one mail on ........., 2014 attaching two letters one for Sri Sankar Jana on ......... 2014 and one for you on ........ 2014 and on ....... 2014, which now revised as mentioned below:-

Before proceeding to Delhi for publication of my Book- **"Evolution of Human Beings and Society"** during last Durga Puja, during .............., 2013 I got message from my Angel that I am going to meet one well wisher who will give me power to solve and fulfill all of my problems and my mission to establish **Bridhyashram**. And that message becomes true when I met Didi, your Wife in the place of Shri Krishna Temple - **"DELHI ISCKON" GUEST HOUSE"** where I also got one single Room booking being a life member. You welcome me in your Room where she gave me full confidence that you will solve all of my problems and listening your appraisals about your contact and influence with **Chief Justice, Mr. ......... of Supreme Court of India** with whom you are joining in weekly meeting also and accordingly I have accepted your all demands without any hesitation for settlement of my individual cases on merit and made 100% advance payment to you for the below mentioned Cases and to the **Publisher, Sri S. J. of B.C.C. /B.T. M.** introduced by your trusted **Commission Agent, Sri S. M.** From your this trusted **Agent** I have come to know that he did arrange huge money (more than Rs.50,000/-) from his parent for you for the last two years to move his parent's Case to Supreme Court from High Court and he also managed to get good amount of commission. My cases are given below for which you have collected huge commission directly and through your **Agent** keeping me as **Hallal Bakra:-**

**1. First** - publication of my Book in three languages for which you have given me your trusted **Group Agent, S. M.** who did arrange one **Publisher, Sri S. J. of M/s B. C. C.** who made me most unhappy after receiving 100% money for three languages of the said Book for 100 copies each including editing, translating, media circulation and launching in Book Fair since ..........., 2013. And from this 100% payment all of you got your share of commission. The said Publisher sent a message through the said Agent that Proof Reading will be ready by ....... 2014. But more than one year running, the **Publisher, Sri S. J.** who is under control of Government's CCTV Camera will not be able to publish my Book. And finally as per your instruction to your Agent who advised me to give one letter which I have given on 31.07.2014 a clearance letter for putting my name, **S. B. as Publisher in place of 'B.C.C.'** but after on priority will be first of finalization of Builder's acceptance of making construction of **Bridhyashram** in our land from Builder's allocation of 55% including my 5% relief given by all owners to me. But he has become **Revenue Cancer Patient** and cannot share his Commission with others, your linked persons who have handed over me as **Hallal Bakra** to **Mr. S.J. of B.C.C.** Mr. S.J. has arranged Financier and Builder for my **Bridhyasram** as **Agent** for earning huge commission out of profit after which he has to share to you and to your Group Agent, Mr. S.M. Now I could realise after joint meeting with Mr. S.J. and Builder, D.B on ..... 2014 that he will prolong his negative attitude for not constructing the **Bridhyshram** and publishing the **Book** till ....... 2015 and ...... 2015, which he uttered in between discussion in the meeting. **On ..........  2014 Mr. S.J.** sent a message to your **Group Agent, S.M.** with a copy to me stating **"Dear Mr. S.M., please discuss with S.B. regarding his Construction. Any voluntary help I'll try my level best. I'll call you ..... 2014. Next sitting time .......... 2014 PM at any venue as per your decision. Please take necessary steps as early as possible. S.J."** On........ Dec. morning I contacted your Group Agent, Mr. S.M. who replied that he doesn't know about the message but he will check and inform me accordingly. Now I am sure that you must have informed your Mr. S. J. Through your Group Agent, S. M. not to process any of my matters.

**2. Second**-Self Construction of my Joint Property Land-Case No.WP/254w submitted on ........... 2013. I was expecting as per your commitments after one or two hearing at least in the month of ........., 2014, I will get the final Order. And I paid you 100% money of Rs............/-. But because of your bad intention, Petition signed by **Adv. N. N. B.**, your senior who did say that he has only signed without going through the petition on receipt of his fees. Next you have given to your Junior without attaching the detailed list of Annexure-'A' & 'B' along with documents and result of which on Motion Date ............ 2014 your Junior, S. S. could not submit his argument and Opponent Parties took the benefit of incomplete petition and did not appear on that date. **Petition filed on ............ 2014 & motion held on ........... 2014.** As per our Younger Brother's report the above petition will not appear in the court as their Advocate managed with manipulation and settlement with you by paying huge lump sum money before submission of this petition. Your junior, Sukanta Sarkar advised by spending Rs.2000/- my case can be put in other

Court where daily position can bring faster result with final order. When I requested him he told that he cannot do if you do not give him permission which I told you and you replied next month that case will be shifted and that way the petition is hanging around for indefinite period. Presently you have managed to keep all of your Senior and juniors in your confidence and instructed not to keep any contact with me and not to attend any of my cases. Now I would request you to please make two money recovery suit, one for construction of Building by my own Licensed Enterprise, M/s S.B.C.Services on our Joint Property Land for which I have already spent totaling to Rs........... up to and including ............ 2014 against two Brothers outstanding comes to Rs............./- for Sri S.B.'s younger Brother and Rs............./- for Sri S. C.B. SB's Elder Brother. Another Recovery suit against Sri S.'s. younger brother for lending Business Loan which now comes to Rs.............- till ............ 2014.

**3. Third** – KWEIL – Kolkata Weir Industries Limited, Diamond Harbour where we have sent our legal notice and acknowledgement received. I have already submitted my Write-up along with Statement of outstanding up to ...... 2014 including Principal based on which we can move to appropriate Consumer Court claiming compensation for monetary hardship and mental torture to one Senior Citizen. **Petition will be submitted on .......... 2014.** Since I have come to know that in this case your one another Agent, Typist sitting in Judges' Court, Alipore, who arranged Advocate after taking all filling matters from me and forced me to pay as per his demands from which he has to pay your commission. And as per your instruction Agent Halder did not follow up for disposal of summon to the opponent parties for which I gave him Rs......../- and further money of Rs........./-to give to filling Officer. When I enquired he was shouting on me saying all summons have been sent don't remind me in time to time. But I did not believe, next day I enquire and paid further Rs..../- to the filling Officer and he immediately dispatched all those summons. Since the above Petition was redrafted and printed by me spending total amount of Rs........./- including Rs......./- paying your Fees and to other Advocates for attending all hearings. Therefore, I have decided to contest my case on my own without contacting your selected Agents.

**4. Fourth** – Cheater, Pannalal Case on.......... 2014 after filling petition No............. of 2014 against P. R. in National Consumers Disputes Redressal Forum with reference of rejected orders of our Petition against P. R. State Consumers Disputes Redressal Forum. All related documents I gave you in the month of ................'14 for filling in State Consumers Disputes Redressal Forum details mentioned in the mail of ............... 2014. In this case I have redrafted, printed and submitted the Petition to you for submission to the Forum for which I have taken your Clerk with me on............. 2014. For both the Petition you have taken signature of **Adv. N. N. B.** But on admission hearing date you could not put up my case properly because you did not study properly therefore the Judge taken 10 days for study and given next admission date on ............. 2014. And he did not listen anything for hearing and straightway given his verdict of rejection. I have spent total Rs............/- including your 100% fees of Rs......../- with all expenses. Next you have decided to put up in National Consumers Dispute Redressal Forum, New Delhi and asked me to join on ........... 2014 to file the above case challenging to the rejected order of State Consumer's Disputes Redressal Forum. As per your typist while coping from my Pen Drive and doing retyping in your presence you have asked him to delete two paragraphs viz Fixed Assets Statement and my First Advocate Notice for payment of my outstanding. While checking retyped petition with the documents I found the above documents deleted that two paragraphs and again I made for inclusion in the petition. Till ......., 2014 I have spent total Rs........./- including additional fees of Rs........./-to you and my expenses for attending the dates of hearing. Out of Rs.7500/- Rs......./- given to you and Rs........./- given to Adv. N. N. B. for Advocate Security by Postal Order which was false requirement when I have come to know from Filling Officer that there is no such requirement for submitting this petition in NCDRF, New Delhi. Factually the further payment of Rs........./- fees was not required when I have already paid in the State Commission. Few days back I have come to know that you have left for Delhi and on hearing such news I am living with anxiety that you must be trying to contact all Opponent Parties to make lump sum deal to massacre my case like my Brothers' case above irrespective of my commitment to pay 5% on total receipts for this case. On .......... 2014, admission date, I was not allowed to be with **Adv. N. N. B.** to listen his hearing version but I have heard that he is requesting for long days to make the documents and the Judge given six and half months e.i. on.............., 2015. Now I would request you to please advise him to give the copy of one Judgment which you showed me on ......., 2014 similar my case and copy of Condonation letter which **Adv. N. N. B**. taken back from me to put up request application for early hearing. I am again confirming by increasing my lump sum payment of 10% after realization of my final receipt amount. If you want I am prepared to sign any agreement on this commitment.

5. **Fifth -Case No. A/C-.........,** Petition submitted on ............ 2007 against J. P. B. for which you have prepared an application consulting 3 and 4 other advocates for contempt of Court under Section 226 of the Constitute Of India in the matter of **S.B.**, Petitioner Versus The State of West Bengal and Officer-In-Charge, Dum Dum Police Station without mentioning the main victim's name, J. P. B. For this you have demanded Rs......./- but while filling the petition you have expressed that I need not be present for filling the petition. So that what will be the outcome is beyond my thinking. For preparing this petition I have spent Rs......./- for collecting certified true copy of total Orders passed on different hearing dates, original of which I have given to you and you are not prepared to give me back. For getting this certified true copy your linked Agent, Sri D.D. w ho demanded Rs......./- because he has to give commission to you. I request you to please rethink about this matter because I am not in a position to spend any further amount on this case. If possible make a money recovery suit.

Thanks and Regards.

c. c.   1.   **Sri N.N.B., Senior Advocate, Supreme Court Bar ssociation, Room No. 1 & C/o Smt. R. Bain,** vill./P.O. Chandpara, P.S. Gaighata, Dist. North 24 Parganas

2. Sri S.D., Advocate, C/o S.B., Rabindra Pally, P.O.Baghajatin, P.S. Patuli, Kolkata-

3. Sri S. J., M/s B.C.C., 1, Indra Roy Road, P.S. Bhowanipur, Kolkata-

4. Sri S.M., C/o Smt. Dolly Mandal, Purbachal Main Road, P.O.Haltu, P.S. Garfa, Kolkata.

# ANOTHER NEW PETITION FILED AGAINST PUBLISHER FOR MAKING MASSACRE OF AUTHOR'S 8TH EDITION OF TWO BOOKS THROUGH PRINTER

IN THE DISTRICT CONSUMER DISPUTES REDRESSAL FORUM AT ALIPORE, 24 PARGANAS (SOUTH), DISTRICT JUDGES COURT, Kolkata - 700027

Consumer Complaint No: …… of 2015

Mr.S Banerjee Son of Late J. K. Banerjee………., residing at Purbachal Main Road, P.O. Haltu, P.S. Garfa, Dist. 24 Parganas (South), Kolkata – 700078…………. Complainant

-Vs-

1………….…..…., Publisher and Editor of M/s …………..
Corporation, Book Publication and Media House, ……….
Road, P.S. ………, Kolkata – 700025

2. Mr………., New Jadavpur …………. Road, P.S………….., Kolkata

3. Mr. ……, Editor/Publisher, ……… House,……….., P.S.-…………….., Kolkata………….…………….. Opposite Parties

**An amendment to this application under Section 11 and 12 of Consumer Protection Act, 1984 valued at Rs…………..../-(Rupees …………………………….)**

Laxmi Nayaran

To

The Hon'ble President and his Companion Members of the District Consumer

Disputes Redressal Forum.

The humble Amendment of Paragraph No.7 of this petition of the Complainant;

Most respectfully Sheweth:

**1.** That your applicant states that in the year 2013, October, during Durga Puja your Applicant had gone to Delhi for publication of revised 7$^{th}$ Edition of his **Book- "Evolution of Human Beings and Society".** While living in New Delhi at "ISCON" Guest House the Applicant met one guest, Smt. ............ Roy, wife of Advocate, Mr.S.D., whom he addressed as Didi, in the same Guest House in Bhog Seva place. The said Didi told your Petitioner that his all problems will be solved by her Husband, Mr.S.D., Advocate, and invited the Petitioner in their Room of ISCON Guest House. The said Advocate, Mr.S.D. first started giving his appraisal of his credential about his high contacts with all senior advocates and highly influential people of Supreme Court of India with whom he used to join in weekly meeting etc.

**2.** That the said Advocate assured the publication of Books- Revised 7$^{th}$ Edition of **"Evolution of Human Beings and Society"** and by calling his Group **Agent, S.M.** inside Calcutta

High Court informing him to introduce the **Complainant** with **Sri ..............., Publisher and Editor, Opposite Party No.1.** They all together share their respective commission from the payments received from parties charging more than double rates of other Publishing Houses' rate. This Publisher, **Opposite Party No.1** does not have his own infrastructure to complete the respective jobs which are done by hired expertise on commission. For the purpose of recording the above statements the **Complainant** sent one Final Request Letter dated ..... 2014 to the **Advocate, S.D.** giving complete details of his extortionate activities in respect of Petitioner's five legal cases including this publication of **Books**. On receipt of this Letter the said Advocate did not send any solution or any contradictory reply to the **Complainant**. Copy of the above Letter attached and marked as **Annexure-A/1.**

**3.** That the **Complainant** submits the followings about the above mentioned **Book- "Evolution of Human Beings and Society"**

a) This Book is written for **80% BPL & APL Categories of People** because democratic Government's Development Activities are only for **20% Burgeon People**. This Book is to make revolution of **Human Culture** to build up **Socialistic Pattern of Society.** Indian Democracy is resisting **Right of Expression.** Some well-wishers of the **Complainant** are warning that the **Complainant** may be kidnapped or taken away from the social atmosphere and thrown to the Encounter Squad to eliminate permanently.

b) The **Complainant** has established one **NGO-"…………..**
**Society"** for arranging **Bridhyashram**for senior citizens
in urban/city and village with cheaper rate where those are
thrown from house or getting ill-treatment from their own
kith and keens without Government's support. As per Sri
………………., **Opposite Party No.1** who expressed present
Government's displeasure about this **Book** and unable to
publish as it is without deleting some matters. About the above
mentioned **NGO- "………….. Society"** got its **Logo's** Trade
Mark Registration Number for which **Sri ………** demanded
Rs…………/- which is more than double as per registered
Agent's rate.

c) The **Complainant** for making this Book strong and
worth accepting sent one copy of this **Book** to One renowned
South Indian Journalist and Writer who is busy in research of
Kolkata History living alone for the last 60 years in Kolkata
for his valuable Foreword. But after ten days he returned those
two Books giving some incidences of democratic torture where
writer like the **Complainant** also cannot live in peace.

**4.** That the **Complainant** through one letter dated…... 2014
addressed to M/s ………… Corporation, Attn. **Sri ……** and
copy to Advocate, S.D., and Sri ……….., **Group Agent** made
a request letter for draft agreement of 100 copies of **Books** in
three languages and change of format. Copy attached marked
as **Annexure A/2 (a)**

**5.** That **Sri ……………, Opposite Party No.1** sent one
e-mail on……… 2014 in reply of the **Complainant** letter

dated ........ 2014 and ................. 2015 & e-mail dated
........... 2014 giving various reasons simply to delay the
process and reluctant attitude for not publishing the Books.
Copy attached and marked as **Annexure-A/2(b)(i-iv)**

**6.** The **Complainant** sent another letters as per advice of
Advocate, S.D. through his **Group Agent**, Sri ......... dated
............... 2014 to **Sri.........., Opposite Party No.1** for
changing publisher name as S. Banerjee, i.e. the **Complainant's**
name who has got ISBN No........ for publishing **Books** in
ten languages in place of M/s Bengal Creative Corporation
on the terms for confirmation and/or acceptance of the
builder/developer for construction of **Bridhyashram** on the
**Complainant's** Joint Property first. Copy attached marked
as **Annexure A/2 (c) (I & ii)**

**7.** That the **Complainant** submits all bad intention of
**Opposite Party No1**. who did engage his **Group Agent**
**Sri................** who reached to the Petitioner's Printer,
Sri.............., New..............., ......... Road, Jadavpur,
Kolkata -700032, **Opposite Party No.2** to delay the printing
process giving obscure Photo of Mahasveta Devi which was
shown earlier to the **Complainant** who did not approve that
photo, to be affixed in her foreword letter replacing the original
affixed photo and also advised the Printer to print the **Book**
totally in black colour including all images after removing
one line "**8TH EDITION – JANUARY 2014**" and to delay
the delivery process. As a result that Sri ...................,
**Opposite Party No.2** is suffering for not getting his final
payment. On .................... 2015 the **Complainant** issued

one advance cheque No. ………. for Rs………/- from his O.D.A/c with SBI, Garfa Branch in favour of Printer for making one copy for Proof Reading after book setting and another Cheque No. ……... drawn on SBI, Garfa Branch for Rs………/- on ………... 2015 for printing and handing over to Binder for binding and next on ……... 2015 the **Complainant** sent a stop payment letter to Bank when he was not getting any responds from Printer's Mobile for informing the total massacre in printing of **Books** on ……... 2015 after taking delivery from the Binder at night. On ……. 2015 the said Printer rang up to the **Complainant** confirming to rectify all the **Books** as per original copied in Pen Drive by Printer, **Opposite Party No.2** from the **Complainant's** Laptop brought in Printer's Office on ………... 2015. As per Printer's request and commitment that he will reprint as per Original, accordingly the **Complainant** did send one E-mail on …………. 2015 attaching his setting proof reading Books including original Photograph of Mahasveta Devi (JPEG & Tiff form). Since the **Complainant** urgently require the reprint of earlier printed 20 Books, the Printer personally came to the **Complainant's** house and taken those 20 **Books** of each **"Indian Democracy" and "Evolution of Human Beings and Society"** on ……... 2015 to be given back to the **Complainant** on or before ………. 2015 before his leaving for Delhi. But there was no responds even after making various mobile calls. Copy of E-mail and above mentioned **Books** attached and marked as **Annexure-A/3 (i-iii).**

**7(a)** On……... 2015 at ……. A.M. spoken 31 seconds by Sri ………., Opposite Party No.2 by his own Mobile No. ……… informing the complainant that he will not return those reprinted Books as per instruction of Mr. ..........., Group Agent of Mr. .........., First Party No.1 through Sri ..............., Principal of M/s ............... Performance', who was earlier known to the Group Agent, Sri.............. when the Complainant was student in the above Institution for computer basic learning and the said Principal came to the Complainant's house for collecting all the Books for reprinting and issuing Receipt on ...... 2015 hand written by the said **Principal, Sri .....................** of 'M/s ............. Performance'on Printer's Letter Head. Accordingly, the Complainant has suffered loss and seeks compensation for Rs................/-. Copy attached and marked as **Annexure-A/3 (i to iii & iv).**

**8.** That there is another incidence while finalizing for publishing the total Books through **Sri ..........,** Editor, ........... Publishing House, ..............., Kolkata-75, **Opposite Party No.3** only for Printing, all others like editing, DTP, cover Page, Banner and binding will be done by the **Complainant**, rate @ Rs......./- for 120 Books each for 22 pages **"Indian Democracy"** and 234 pages **"Evolution of Human Beings and Society"** for printing, launching and selling at Publisher's Stall No..... in Kolkata Book fare from .............. 2015 @ 35% commission. After taking Book setting Printout and handing over to **Sri ............, Opposite Party No.3**, the **Complainant** requested for draft agreement for finalizing the above Books in three languages. But he did not give that draft agreement and finally putting the **Complainant's** own name as Publisher, the **Complainant** given for Printing to Printer, **Opposite Party No.2**. But **Sri ..............., Opposite Party**

**No.3** of knowledge Publishing House has taken 5 copies of each Book with one Banner for displaying in his Stall No...... in Kolkata Book Fare and in Stall No.......... in Delhi Book Fare for selling. The **Complainant** witnessed the displayed **Books** in both the Book Fare in Kolkata and Delhi. But there is no news of selling Books. When tried to contact, there is no responds. It is cleared that **Group Agent, Sri..........** must have influenced through some high link and managed to massacre the **Complainant's** publishing efforts. Copy of the Receipt attached herewith and marked as **Annexure-A/4**

9.  That the **Complainant** for record purpose given one copy to Assistant Library and Information Officer was sitting in Publishing Guild House of Kolkata Book Fare on ......... 2015 vide their Memo No............./2015, Government of India, National Library mentioning the Book stall No....... After reprint the **Complainant** will replace this **Book** giving the New One. The copy of the Memo is attached herewith and marked as **Annexure-A/5**

10. That the **Complainant** submits that herein he was subjected to false promises and inhuman tortures for not publishing the **Books** and constructing the **Bridhyashram** on the **Complainant's** joint properties.

a) On ......... 2014 the **Opposite Party No.1** sent through his **Group Agent**, Sri ............ schedule of publishing date on various writers in Bengali languages in which the **Complainant's Books** will be published on ............. 2014 and on ........ 2014 convocation will be held where the

**Complainant's** name also mentioned but Invitation Card was not sent. Copy attached and marked-**Annexure-A/6**

b) On ......... 2014/...... 2014- the **Complainant** sent one letter and E-mail of corrected message in reply of message through mobile call during ........., 2014 from Respondent No.1 regarding schedule of meeting on ....., 2014 sent to SRi....."" with a copy to the **Complainant** for finalization of construction of **Bridhyashram** and publishing of **Books**. Copy of these documents attached with **Annexure–A/7**

**11.** That on ........ 2015/...... 2015 the **Complainant** sent one letter by Speed Post and by E-mail recollecting all incidences on ........ 2015 advanced arranged Joint Meeting by the **Opposite Party No.1** in his Office that how he made a plan as advised by the said **Advocate, Sri S.D.** shown in **Annexure A/1** to forfeit the whole money of the **Complainant** by preparing one letter in Bengali language on his own hand writing addressed to his name- Sri .............., Road, Kolkata-25 that is his concocted own Self Confession Statement for closing the Petitioner's Revised 7th Edition **Book- "Evolution of Human Beings and Society"** taking the **Complainant's** signature as if the **Complainant** is writing to him giving all various information for which the **Complainant** has no knowledge and evidence without giving any copy to the **Complainant**. On trust and belief the **Complainant** signed the letter but when the **Complainant** asked for about **8th Edition** then the **Opposite Party No.1** cut a sorry remark and tear of the letter in two pieces for making new Letter. Since the care taker was insisting to close the Main gate at an early hour for the day being the Saturday, the said letter was not prepared. Next the **Complainant** requested the **Opposite Party No.1** to sign the certificate of Editor as written "EDITED BY – Sri …….., …… Corporation, ……… Road, Bhowanipur, P.S.…….., Kolkata-25 (Certified with full confidence that the Author's views and opinions are fully authentic as per news paper Reports and personal verification of various incidences) in the attached copy of sheet (ii) of the **Book** carried with the **Complainant** on …… 15. For this Certificate the **Opposite Party No.1** has taken the **Complainant's** Company's Visiting Card which mentioned the **Complainant's** Rank and Position details with company's address and telephone numbers, Original Card attached. Also own hand written foreword letters' copies of Mahasevta Devi, and late Neepesh Chandra Talukder, IAS, Retired member of Posts and Telegraph Board, Government of India, New Delhi given to **Sri ……………, Opposite Party No.1.** On this matter the **Opposite Party No.1** made one drama by calling his Advocate Mr. …….. for taking his concurrence and given that Mobile to the **Complainant** for confirming that he cannot give such certificate and when I was enquiring that Advocate's credential The **Opposite Party No.1** immediately snatched the Mobile and did not sign the Certificate. On ………. 2015 the Opposite Parties' Group Agent, Sri…………. kept one envelope attaching the concocted letter in Letter Box of the **Complainant.** All letters copies attached and marked as **Annexure-A/8(i-iv)**

12. **Annexure A/9** - That your **Complainant** submits the following details of transactions with Sri………….., **Opposite Party No.1** date-wise. Whereby the **Complainant** informed

the said **Opposite Party No.1** about his hard earned money and in as much as other valuable loans.

a) On ......... 2013 the **Complainant** had requested Sri ........, **Opposite Party No.1** for publishing his 7th Revised Edition **Book- "Evolution of Human Beings and Society"** in three languages.

b) On......... 2013 Publisher, Sri Sankar Jana's acceptance letter in Bengali on **Complainant's** above request letter.

c) (i) ........... 2013 Quotation and advance Receipt for:. T.P./Layout/editing harges vide Cheque No....... drawn on SBI, Garfa, Branch.......... Rs......../-

(ii) Advance for 100 copies of two Books in English & in Bengali vide Cheque No........... drawn on SBI, Garfa Branch.................. Rs............./-

(iii) Advance for 100 copies of the above Book in Hindi vide Cheque No.......... drawn on SBI, Garfa Branch ................. Rs........./- iv) .......... 2013 Quotation and full payment for publicity vide Cheque No........... drawn on SBI, Garfa Branch (Receipt not given)...................... Rs............../-

(v)....... 2013 Publisher's own use Perfect Software linked with M/s GOLDTEK advised me to pay cash vide Bill/Receipt No.nil dated.......... 2013 Rs........./- Total Rs.........../-

All copies and Bank A/c Statements attached marked as **Annexure A/9-{a, b, c (i to v)}**

(d)  That the **Complainant** wrote to the **Opposite Party No.1** on ....... 2014/......... 2014 for printing of 20 copies of English Book - **"Evolution of Human Beings and Society"** requesting for urgent print for distribution of copies to dignitaries but he did not respond. Hence the **Complainant** had incur expenses for the printing which costs as per rate of the **Opposite Party No1**@ Rs........../-) per Book for 20 copies-)-Rs............/-

All copies of letters attached and marked as **ANNEXURE-A/9 (d)**

(e)  That the **Complainant** by his letter dated .......... 2015 requested **Opposite Party No.1** to transfer Rs........./- to Petitioner's SB A/c with SBI, Garfa Branch giving IFSC No... for publishing/printing of **8th Edition** after changing Publisher Name, 120 copies for launching in Kolkata Book Fair on ................., 2015 @ Rs......./- Above letter attached and marked as **Annexure-A/9(e)......................** Rs....../-

(f)  That the **Complainant** Includes interest for the period from ......... 2013 to.............. 2015, copies of Bank Statements attached and marked as **Annexure-A/9/f (i-ii).....** Rs................/-

(g)  That the **Complainant** includes his share of 30% Royalty on Rs.........................................) as per Publisher rate......................... Rs............./-

(h) "That the **Complainant** needs compensation for inhuman torture, mental agony, loss of reputation @Rs....../- per month and Rs....../- Bank loan Interest for construction of Bridhyshram/Old-Age-Home per month totaling to Rs....../- per month for 8 months from August'14 to March'15 amounting to ........................ Rs............/-Total amount - **A/9 (a to h)**............. Rs.........../-. And this monthly compensation of Rs............./- needs to be carried forward till the final settlement".

**13.** That finding no other alternative Your **Complainant** made a legal notice on ......... 2015 to **Sri Sankar Jana,** the **Opposite Party No.1** requesting to consider the refund of amount within 15 days from the date of the date of receipt of the said notice but the **Opposite Party No.1** even after receipt of the said notice, failed and neglected to refund said amount within the stipulated period. Xerox copy of this notice attached with **Sl.No.13** and marked as **Annexure-A/10**

**14.** That Your **Complainant** states that for non-payment of deposited amount to your **Complainant** the cause of action of this complaint has first arisen from.............. 2013, .......... 2014 /......... 2014 and ........... 2015 and thereafter when **Complainant** made a legal notice on ........ 2015 upon the **Opposite Party No.1** for refund of money to your **Complainant** and the same has been continuing till date at .........., Purbachal Main Road, Kolkata –78, which is within the jurisdiction of your Hon'ble Forum.

**15.** Your **Complainant** submit that unless the prayer herein below is not allowed the **Complainant** will suffer irreparable loss and injury.

**16.** For the purpose and jurisdiction of the Hon'ble Forum the Court fees of Rs............/- is paid vide Draft............/- in favour of The President, District Consumer Disputes Redressal Forum, Alipore, Kolkata-27, South 24 Parganas, west Bengal is paid thereon accordingly. Under the circumstances above, it is most humbly  prayed that your honour would graciously be pleased to:

a)  Pass necessary order to refund the deposit amount to the **Complainant** e.i........................... Rs.............../-

b)  Pass an order to repay the total cost paid by the **Complainant** for DTP & Printing..................... Rs.................../-

c)  Pass an order for 30% Royalty on Rs.........../- ................
Rs........./-

d)  Pass an order for O.D. Interest @10.50 on Rs........../- for 15 months........... Rs. ....../-

e)  Pass an order for inhuman torture, mental agony and loss of Reputation @ Rs........./-per month and non fulfillment of construction of Bridhyshram @Rs............/- per month up to ............. 2015 for Rs. ........................./- and Rs........../- per month to be made till final settlement.

f) Pass an order for giving the Editing Certificate - "Edited by Sri ......... Consultant of ..................... Corporation,.......... Road, .............. Bhowanipur P.S., Kolkata-25 (Certified with full confidence that the Author's views and opinions are fully authentic as per news paper Reports and personal verification of various incidences)

g) Pass an order for reprinting and binding of 120 Books of **"Evolution of Human Beings and Society" And "Indian Democracy"** after rectifying all changes as per original Script and colour of 5 images of first Book and two images of second Book to be done by **Sri Anup Kumar Datta, New Jadavpur Art Press, Printer.** And failing which Sri Anup Kumar Datta should pay the compensation Rs........./- to the Complainant.

h) Pass an order for returning 5 Books of each of **"Indian Democracy" and "Evolution of Human Beings and Society"** including Banner by Sri ..............., Editor of .............. Publishing House

# SAMPLE LETTERS FOR SYSTEM TO MAKE CORRUPTION FREE GOVERNANCE BY KMC

**The Assessor/Collector,**
**The Kolkata Municipal Corporation, Jadavpur**
**Unit, Santoshpur Market, (3ʳᵈ Floor),**
**Santoshpur Avenue, Kolkata – 700075**

**Sir,**

## SUB: REQUEST TO ISSUE TAX CLEAREENCE CERTIFICATE FOR PTREMISES NO....ESSESSEE NO.......

While on the subject I have submitted all relevant tax paid receipts and earlier Tax Clearance Certificates in original issued on .......... and on ........ against our above mentioned two premises. But concerned officer, who is issuing Tax Clearance Certificate, again issued LOI dated........... for payment of difference for an amount of Rs........, which has been paid by me on ........ Likewise I paid earlier LOI payment of Rs...... on ........ for Tax Clearance Certificate twice on the same Assessed No......... I am further submitting herewith all the relevant receipts pertaining to years from 1995 to 1999 for your kind checking and refund.

After payment of LOI, concerned officer advised me to go to the Dy. Assessor/Collector to request for issuing Tax Clearance Certificate on manual system instead of On Line System. But Dy. Assessor insisted for GR which was pending for two subsequent periods of ..... 2001-2002 and 2/2007-2008 for Assessed No.......... and for Assessed No.......... or period of ......./2007-2008. This GR process took more than a month. When Inspector came to inspect both the Premises, status quo was same as it was in the year 2007 when last Tax Clearance Certificate was issued. I did receive the notice of hearing date for GR on.......... On the same day after completion of GR hearing process in the Cabin of Hearing Officer where the Inspector and one Accounts Officer was also present with all their calculation sheet that was beyond my understanding. Later on I found my appeal to the Hearing Officer gone in vain when I have received the **RATE CARD** and Property Tax-Supplementary Bill of Annual Valuation which has increased 4 times higher than earlier Rate of Rs........ for Assessed No..... and for Assessed No........ present valuation become almost double than earlier Rate of Rs...... Supplementary Bill copy also attached herewith. However, the concerned Tax Clearance Certificate Issuing Officer did confirm me that generally after GR annual valuation increases 10% only. I am constrained to high light the incidence occurred in the cabin of Dy. Assessor in front of few accounts people on............... stating herein below:

After entering in Dy. Assessor's Cabin I tried to convince him for issuance of Tax Clearance Certificate on manual system to get the certificates early to hand over the premises to the Builder/Promoter for constructing Bridhyashram for which I have registered one NGO and applied for 80G for donation. In support of **Bridhyashram** I have shown them one Banner of my own published Book- "**Evolution of Human Beings and Society**" incorporating one letter addressed to Prime Minister sent on ...... for launching in Book Fare from

............. to......... In that letter I have mentioned 99% people are vitiated under control of self centered power crazy dirty politicians. I am attaching this Book and copy of letters to Prime Minister for your kind perusal. This Book is in Part - I and Part-II based on true story of **SB (Sukumar Banerjee)** whose one of the miseries mentioned in page....... & ........ of Part-II for mutation in Kolkata Municipal Corporation (people named "Chorporation") mentioned in page No.... of Part-I of this Book. Like **SB,** I have also become worst victim under the governance of Kolkata Municipal Corporation. To maintain the cleaned and disciplined governance of **KMC** like commercial organization I feel that the autonomous **KMC** Act should be amended as mentioned below:

1. All employees will be given Electronic Punching Card to enter in the office in time to maintain the disciplined attendance.

2. Smoking should be totally banned in the office premises where non-smoking people become sick during the time they remain in the office for business transactions. For unavoidable circumstances, smoking people should use Lavatory Area only.

3. In the office, there should be one Customer Care Centre where new people should seek help for completing the required subject matter without consulting agents who demands 3 to 4 times money on actual cost of each subject matter. These agents distribute 25% money under the table of concerned officer from extra money they collect from customer and 75% retained by them. **I feel entrance of all agents in the**

**office premises and their authorization be abandoned immediately.** Under the unavoidable circumstances if land owner unable to present himself in the **KMC** office can authorize his next nearest relative with proper ID proof and/or alternative that land owner can request over phone or letter to the customer care centre to provide person on chargeable basis. Under the above circumstances, may I request your good self to be kind enough to consider my case sympathetically and give proper justice so that I can proceed for constructing the proposed **Bridhyashram?**

Thanking you, Yours truly,

## 2ND LETTER TO ASSESSOR COLLECTOR

**Sir,**

### SUB: SUBMISSION OF
### "PROPERTY - INFORMATION FORM"

This is as per Times of India Publication of dated.........
Undersigned could collect the above mentioned Form from
your Head Office on....... and as advised by the Assessor/
Collector I am enclosing herewith the said Form duly filled in
for your kind perusal with a request to issue me a fresh bill to
enable me make the payment at the earliest.

While on the subject I am enclosing herewith the copies
of the following letters/documents for giving me sufficient tax
relief from the pending accumulated huge amount of tax even
after clearing my last year dues as per duplicate bill.

1. Copy of TOI publication dated .... on the subject
   matter
2. Copy of letter dated......... to the Assessor/Collector
3. Copy of letter dated....... to the Municipal
   Commissioner
4. Copy of last year Tax paid Receipts dated..........
5. Tax Clearance Certificate dated...... Original taken
   by the Officer of the Department

Thanking you,

**The Municipal Commissioner,**
**The Kolkata Municipal Corporation,**
**Central Municipal Office Building,**
**5, S. N. Banerjee Road,**
**Kolkata – 700013**

Sir,

## SUB: REVISED FIFTH EDITION OF MY BOOK - "EVOLUTION OF HUMAN BEINGS AND SOCIETY"

Submit with all humility that I have made a humble attempt to portray in the Book captioned above, copy enclosed, and the malice which has gripped our 'Mahan Bharat'. I have also brought out the sufferings of senior citizens, who need succour and assistance, without further loss of time.

I appeal to you to spare a little time to glance through my Book, and advise me as to how to reach our people to make them acquainted with malice of the Society, the pitiable condition of senior citizens and remedial measures to be taken by providing one NGO for starting construction of **Bridhyashram /'Old-Age Home'**.

After strenuous efforts, I could manage to register one **NGO Society** and obtained for 80G so that I can serve all senior citizens like me who has become worst victim like **SB** explain in this captioned **Book** for starting construction of 'Old-Age Home'.

Presently I am again in the trap of established malice in the Kolkata Municipal Corporation, Santoshpur Branch when I have shown my Book captioned above printed in one banner incorporating my letter to the Prime Minister............ in the presence of Dy. Assessor and his accounts staff members. I have already forwarded my complain to the Assessor/Collector, Santoshpur Branch under cover of my letter dated............, a copy of which is attached herewith for your kind perusal. This Kolkata Municipal Corporation seems to be the First State Government's, autonomous Commercial Organization in the country, is running 135 years with lot of loopholes in the KMC Act, 1980 to give clearance of all illegitimate claim through KMC judicial proceedings. Simple example of one complaint against my neighbour, Sri.............. who has constructed building without following KMC Rules and encroaching my land but the Judge passed the following orders in favour of P.R. on benefit of doubt ignoring the demolition sketch and various defects prepared by KMC Building Department. 1. P.R. should obtain certificate from KMC paneled L.B.S. for non-violation of KMC rules and 2. Furnish an affidavit and declaring on oath that he will not make any constructions whatsoever in the impugned premises without prior sanction from KMC authority. But the said P.R. has constructed another floor and came to me to utilize my land for south side plastering and colouring since he has not left single inch land for standing in south side. A certified Xerox copy of judgment order without foot note received by me on payment of Rs.400/- is attached herewith. With due respect I would like to draw your kind attention to my captioned Book from pages............ where **SB (Sukumar Banerjee)** has suggested for cleaned and disciplined governance by introducing self -government system. From Block label to District label by new elected people on yearly basis without interference of any political party for administering the following activities under **KMC**.

1. **Revenue/Finance:-a)** Corporation Tax, collecting process fees etc. which brings harassments with heavy penalty in cash under the table to the tax payers mentioned in the letter dated...... addressed to the Assessor/collector copy enclosed. **b)** Sanction of Building Plan:-where LBS demands extra money in addition of normal tariff to satisfy the KMC building engineers for plan sanction and construction certification on inspection. **c)** Other various services staffs demand some Kharchapani in addition to the normal charges.

2. **Roads, Lighting, water Supply, Education, and Health:**

a) First of all we must establish our own Maintenance Department employing our own technicians from Block/Word label instead of giving contract to any third party, where huge pilferage created and result of which bad workmanship, bad quality of materials, nonpayment to the workmen as per minimum wages Act which make a big hole of expenditures. Every year small little roads are broken to replace pipe made out of china clay. Why should we not make permanent concrete pipe.

b) **Road construction and cleaning: -**

i) Construction of roads should be ecliptic type sloping from centre with underground drainage system in both sides of the road and sufficient extra coal tar enamel to be put after concreting by asphalt mixtures for smooth flow of rain water both side of the road.

By this we can stop water stagnancy on the road and damages of road in every rainy season.

ii) **Cleaning of road:** We should install permanent big size HDP Garbage Storage Tank within the distance of 5 to 10 Electric Poles from where automatic garbage collecting motor vehicles will pick up the garbage and throw to the dumping yard. All the above works we are getting through contractors and all skilled civil workers have become contractor but they are now no interest in daily rate basis work. Now they are earning 4 to 5 times more than one-day rate. For sanction of Building Plan, contractor has to apply to Building Department. Next, he has to satisfy Engineer through some assistant and/ or representative of political parties. Next for approving bill, he has to satisfy another engineer. Next, for collecting payment, he has to satisfy cash department and after satisfying all, he has to add his profit to arrive the price of unit of particular work. What will be the cost of the work comparing with our own maintenance department? This is a short description of pilferage.

Sir! If you read my letter to Prime Minister,……. you will find that my calculation is very clear about 99% people are vitiated directly or indirectly under control of self centered power crazy dirty politicians.

Thanking you for your kind and sympathetic consideration towards me to construct **Bridhyashram (Old-Age-Home)** in the existing land.

Yours truly,

# 2ND LETTER TO THE COMMISSIONER

## SUB: REVISED FIFTH EDITION OF MY BOOK - "EVOLUTION OF HUMAN BEINGS AND SOCIETY"

At first I express my heartiest congratulation for your new assignment from when I met you on ............. with my humble letter along with the above captioned Book of 3<sup>rd</sup> Edition for your kind forward addressed to your highness-**"The District Magistrate, South 24 Parganas, Alipore, Kolkata"**.

This captioned Book is now revised incorporating few sample letters and one foreword of **Mother Mahasweta Devi, recipient of Jnanpith and Raman megsayasay award,** which has been affixed with **PREFACE**.

Like **SB,** I am also one of the victims, who could not fulfill his father's wish to make **Bridhyashram (Old-Age-Home)** due to extreme adamant attitude of Sri .........., Dy. Assessor/Collector for Ward No........ from .......... Office, who did convince Assessor/Collector, Sri ............... from same Office to reject my appeal and also told me that Mayor cannot make any changes in the KMC Act established in the year 1876 and the said dy. Assessor is not bound to implement any new method. Accordingly, he has sent my appeal to Head Office. After giving last call to Sri..............., Assessor/ Collector on........... And, next day I met him in the Office when he told that my appeal has not been accepted and Dy. Assessor/ Collector will be sending me a letter which has not yet reached in my address even after visiting the Office continuously for 3 days. I am enclosing herewith the copy of my letter addressed to Assessor/Collector dated ......... along with all relevant documents mentioned below enclosed with the letters.

1. Copy of TOI publication dated....... on the Subject matter
2. Copy of letter dated.......... to the assessor /Collector
3. Copy of letter dated........ to the Municipal Commissioner
4. Copy of last year Tax paid Receipt dated... as per old rate.
5. Tax Clearance Certificate dated......., Original taken by the Officer of the Department.

Very recently one incidence happen for amalgamation of one plot together with another plot of two brothers just attached with our KMC Premise No....... eastern side, Dy. Assessor/ Collector did harass as per his capacity then referred to Asstt. Collector /Assessor after both assessors discussing internally with each other referred the Case to the Accounts Department. Accounts Department after discussing internally with all the executives advised the party to pay cash of Rs.10,000/- and after payment Builder /Promoter got the amalgamation Certificate.

Every time when I did refer earlier Tax Clearance Certificate which confirmed tax paid up to ............ and thereafter tax paid up to last bill of ............... as per same earlier rate then how annual value increase 4 times including earlier years arrears after 2 GR. When statues que of the land remain same as it was in the year ....... as per Tax Clearance

Certificate till date and the above Dy. Assessor/Collector has replied me that I have attended the hearing date. On hearing date……….. Hearing Officer has collected the papers from Inspector and accountant who clarified Officer's queries and said ok but I have not been asked anything and not given any paper to know what is the outcome. Simply I was told to collect my supplementary Bill from billing Section. This is happen in my case due to one incidence happen in his cabin while showing one Banner of my own published Book details of which are mentioned in the attached letter dated………. to the Assessor/Collector of Santoshpur Market Office. This **KMC** Office is established corrupted unit in this City. Hearing Officer is preoccupied with monthly some extra money other than salary. Accordingly, on hearing date agent will satisfy all the executives collecting money from the assessed 4 times of the actual as per **KMC** Rule.

Earlier letters I have given some remedial measures to remove corruption but no changes are visible. Now I feel the following systems only can remove the corruption of **KMC**:-

1. Hearing Officers' post should declare redundant and Hearing Office should close the function.

2. All Agents' entry should abandon. There should be Customer Care Centre to solve all problems and get relief from the harassment by all KMC executives.

3. Entire execution should be under E-Governance System so that customers need not come to KMC Office for any matter which they can gather through Internet, T.V. Channel, local

Broadcasting, and Mobile etc. to avoid penalty or cash under the table for delay due to non receipt of Bill/Communication.

4. To keep City clean and pollution free KMC should introduce own maintenance faculty with own technical expert, materials procurement and storage facility instead of engaging contractors for bad workmanship, rotten materials and pushing money to all the departments for job certification, passing Bill and collecting payments with profit. One simple example, every year after rainy season over new asphalting Road we find that the stone chips are coming out when vehicles are running on the Road or sudden raindrops make a whole on the Road. Reason after asphalting sufficient extra Coal Tar Enable was not given over the new asphalt Road. In the Book, 'SB' had suggested Road construction and cleaning method. As per colour Code of Kolkata City- "White and Blue" Trident Lamp Post without any colour where in the Post should be white and top Cap should be Blue. As such this is another huge amount of corruption        possibly while awarding the contract proper competitive quotation must not have been called for and without auditing such a huge amount of contract has been awarded. In 6th Edition of the captioned Book **"SB"** has given his observation that 60% CPM Cadres working in **KMC** are still busy in party's works and do not maintain service work rule honestly. Now I would request your kind help to give me total relief and show me to how I will be able to construct the **Bridhyashram** to serve **apartheid senior citizens** in the present society. Being a secretary of the **NGO**-................. I have prepared one proposal in Bengali language, copy enclosed, for taking signature of the neighbors

if I get your certificate of total relief from all charges/taxes etc. for mutation, amalgamation and sanction of plan for all the individual land owners.

Thanking you,

Laxmi Nayaran

**The Municipal Joint Commissioner,**
**The Kolkata Municipal Corporation,**
**Central Municipal Office Building,**
**5 S. N. Banerjee Road,**
**Kolkata-700013**

Sir,

**SUB: TAX CLEARENCE CERTIFICATE**
**FOR PREMISES NO........................**
**OF ASSESSEE ............**
**NOC FOR CONSTRUCTION OF BRIDHYASHRAM**

So long, I have been communicating the subject matter through my personal Letter Head and now being the Secretary of **NGO-..................** I am writing this letter in the **NGO's** Letter Head. On..............., while discussing on the subject matters with reference to my reply to Joint Secretary to the Chief Minister and a copy to the Commissioner of Kolkata Municipal Corporation, you did ask me about my attendance on Hearing date on ............ as all other Executives did ask me in every meeting. Every time everywhere my reply was yes but I was not allowed to speak anything since no body asks me anything. Next on receipt of Supplementary Bills I got shock and reported to Dy. Assessor/Collector, ............... who was ready with the Axe for throwing towards me, which I reported in my letter dated .............. attached with my another letter dated ......... addressed to Assessor/Collector for submission of new **"PROPERTY-INFORMATION REPORT"** for revised new Bill. On ...... when I met Sri ........., Assessor/Collector to enquire about the outcome of my submission of New Form for revised Tax Calculation then Sri……….. called for Sri …… and when enquired the status Sri ……. replied that he has sent a letter to my address which was wrong reply. But Sri …… realized the matter then he asked him give him a copy and I have been told to wait outside. After an hour he did prepare the letter/Memo No……. dated ……. which I received on the same day on …… from the dispatch Department, which I did attach with my letter addressed to Sri ……… I.A.S., Joint Commissioner, Kolkata Municipal Corporation on ………. In this Memo No…… dated ……. **The last Paragraph- "But, we regret to inform you that as per the direction of the appropriate authority, there is hardly any scope to reconsider the matter which please note".** Considering some hope, I did again talk to Sri ……. who then told Sri …… to send the file to Head Office. On ……, I could recollect some of the conversation between Sri …… and Sri ………… that some signature is there in the documents, which I did not realize about which documents they were talking about. I am afraid that on Hearing documents Sri ……… must have managed to copy my signature from my submitted documents available in…… KMC Office by Scanning/Xeroxing my signature as per advice of **CM (R)** I am very much conversant with the British made **KMC Act.** But **Sri ………, CM (R)** of Kolkata Municipal Corporation is Super Expert British made **'Dewan'** for Kolkata City. This KMC Act governed by Autonomous Body, parallel Government like State Government. It has got own Judicial system. That is why **CM (R)** always threaten to the Complainant that your case will be sent to Tribunal. I have plenty of instances given below of their huge cash transactions on the table and/or under the table:-1. Sri......, Complainant, residing at ........ Vs. Sri.........., residing at........ before Sri ......, W.B.H.J.S. (Rtd.), Spl. Officer (Bldg.) KMC Demolition Case No......., Br. XII K.M.C. for unauthorized construction and encroachment of our gifted land. Judgment Order passed for Complainant to go to Civil Court within 30 days from the date of order and for P.R. to pay penalty and go ahead for further construction at the end of the last line Xerox of which not given to the Complainant. After Judgment Complainant came to know, that P.R. did spend quite a good amount of cash money in the Department.

**Hearing Section in Revenue Department:** Hearing Officer on deputation from outside Government Department monthly booked for deciding concession, discount, penalty etc. as per Inspector and Accounts People's advice guided by the Assessor/Collector, Dy. Assessor/Collector and other Top Executives. Under this process, huge cash transactions accumulated for full filling the State Government's requirement, Ministers', leaders and others. Unauthorized Encroachment of other Properties is legalized by fabricating documents. There also huge cash transaction took place.

1. Building Department: Only KMC Paneled LBS will submit the Plan as per KMC Rule, who only knows how much percentage of cash transactions are involved after normal Fees by receipt.

2. Other Departments: Delay charges by cash for not clearing dues in time for non-receipt of Bill. But Sri ........, being the Secretary of **NGO- .......** will not get any concession and/or

**NOC for Bridhyashram** due to his discloser of all the above anomalies/corruptions of KMC to the Joint Secretary to the Chief Minister and to the Chief Justice of India, Supreme Court through various letters. Also through his own published **Book-Evolution of Human Beings and Society**. Thanking you for your kind and sympathetic special consideration for **Tax Clearance Certificate as per old rate for one year** and **NOC for Bridhyashram** as per Proposal already submitted to you.

Yours truly,

Laxmi Nayaran

**Member of Lagislative Assembly of West Bengal,
Jadavpur Constituecy, 20 Suren Tagore Road,
Kolkata - 700019**

**Sir,**

## THROUGH CHIEF MINISTER OF WEST BENGAL

### SUB: SEVENTH EDITION OF MY
### BOOK-"EVOLUTION OF
### HUMAN BEINGS AND SOCIETY"
### "Maa, Mati & Manush"

I am blind supporter of the above-mentioned slogan and in support of this slogan; I am enclosing herewith my own published Book mentioned above and copy of following letters for your kind perusal.

1. Copy of Letter to Prime Minister of India along with copy of acknowledgement from his Chief Secretary addressed to Chief Secretary of Chief Minister of West Bengal with a copy to me.
2. Copy of letter to General Secretary of west Bengal Communist Party of India (Marxist), Kolkata.
3. Copy of Chief Justice of India, Supreme Court of India, Delhi.

After Election, all Elected Leaders are available in protected place where any individual cannot meet for expressing his views/suggestions/complaints for living better life in the Society under **Burgeon Platform of Anarchism/ Nepotism of 20%**

**Burgeon People without fear and anxiety**. I have explained in the second Letter addressed to the General Secretary of west Bengal Communist Party of India (Marxist) how this **Burgeon Platform** is established.

As I understand, Government is now in financial crux position and members' Development Funds are not sufficient to develop any individual Block development works in your Constituency. There is only one Real Estate Business place available where maximum profit margin can be extracted from the Builders/Promoters Account. I have two Blocks for construction of **Bridhyashram** i.e.

1. My own Proposal of Seven Plots measuring about 4 Bighas in our Block of Ward No106 and another one in Bhadreswar, Hooghly, Proposal already given to Joint Secretary of Ministry of Home i.e.

2. **Second Plot under Bhadreswar Municipality ............ with my One Cheater, Sri Chitterlal who is living in this Plot with his mother, against whom I have filled a suit U/s ........ for not paying my due mount against Loan paid from my Bank Over-Draft A/c with .......... on Interest of 12%, 11.5% and 10.75%. This Cheater has tremendous influence with Marwari Business Communities and with various Senior Advocates.**

As per suggestions in first letter to Prime Minister 20% from net profit of Builders/ Promoters' Account after keeping some Reserve Fund for warranty/maintenance period. As per my Book and our NGO, systems of running **Bridhyashram** actual plus 10% for Reserve Fund without any profit margin. However, I require additional Reserve Fund for Health Care Centre for Senior Citizens due to which profit margin of Builders/Promoters will be reduced. Since, I have already agreed to the Club Executives that I will fulfill their demand of 10% from 20% booking money from Promoter's Allocation. I wish to deposit this money to Chief Minister's Relief Fund and/or Chief Minister's Development Fund directly instead of Club Executives. In this Constituency under Borough-XII, one Hospital is there near Vivekanada Road. If Government can reconstruct this Hospital with up to date modern amenities and ICU OT facility with all pathological diagnostics, physiotherapy etc. Reconstruction of this Hospital required various approach Roads from northern side. If this Hospital is available then Reserve Fund for our NGO Health Care Centre could be synchronized with lesser amount. As per commitment of **Shri …….. Club Executives and TMC Block In-Charge,** who confirmed that he would conduct joint meeting with all Land Owners in 3rd week of October'13 and accordingly I have withdrawn the Criminal Case under Section 406 & 420 against my two Brothers for not allowing me to construct the Building on ……... Cottahs of land @40/60 ratio and business loan to my younger Brother to clear my debt of Rs……........ from O.D. Accounts. I shall be obliged to receive your approval and directive to the Club Executives to enable me to start mobilization activities on our Block. And for Second one, clearance from Commissioner of Bhadreswar Municipality.

Thanking you,
'Yours truly,

**General Secretary of West Bengal Communist Party of India, Office of the Communist Party of India (Marxist) 31 Alimuddin Street, Kolkata - 700019**

**Sir!**

If we recollect our patriarch of **CPM Party,** whose confession in the year 2000 in the TV Channel that our **CPM Party** could not establish socialistic pattern of Society while taking over the reign of this State due to Self-centered Power Crazy mentality, which could not over turn the existing **Burgeon ruling Platform of 20% people of total population.** Present Government Party took reign of this State by changing **Slogan "Maa, Maati and Manush"** on the same **Burgeon ruling Platform** which will prove to be **Vague Slogan.** All leaders/ Ministers are busy to keep their Power intact by arranging Funds in corrupt way and/or by unfair means engaging all bureaucrats, **Cadres/Workers** to meet the Party's expenditures. Now as per **SB's** advice I appealed to all political parties joining together to make one new **Third Front Group** to take the reign of this Country and the State for betterment of **80% BPL & APL Categories of people**.

Yours truly,

Laxmi Nayaran

# 2ND LETTER TO:

**General Secretary of West Bengal Communist Party of India, Office of the Communist Party of India (Marxist) 31 Alimuddin Street, Kolkata - 700019**

Respected Sir,

## SUB: SEVENTH EDITION OF MY BOOK-<u>EVOLUTION OF HUMAN BEINGS AND SOCIETY"</u>

I am being a permanent supporter of CPM Party have right to request/circulate for self criticism for not complying the philosophy/ideology of Marxism for the welfare of proletariat, **APL, BPL categories of people who are 80%** of our country's total population.

During 34 years ruling in our State all our power crazy self-centered elected leaders worked as First Category of King as Administrative King to serve **20% Burgeon People** living in the Cities or in the developed villages extracting money from the Business Communities as Financial Kings controlling the entire economy of the State and the Country as a whole. During the last 34 years ruling we have changed human culture to survive in the society of Anarchism/Nepotism under the shed of unlimited Democracy by force, unfairness, looting, cheating, etc supported by leaders and their administrative forces. Humanity, honesty etc. eradicated from the human mind. Entire bureaucratic systems did make a concrete Platform for extracting money under the direction of all self-centered power crazy leaders. The best example is now Kolkata Municipal Corporation where about 60% people are belonging to **CPM/Leftists Party** and most of them are busy in party's campaign.

Now I have become the worst victim coming after 40 years from exile for keeping my service alive on transfer out of Bengal in the year 1966 when a political party was trying to capture the reign of this state by destroying the industries and business atmosphere of this State by slogan, procession, strike etc. Presently I am living alone in a single room of my parental house in Block No….. of ward No…… where in I am planning to construct Bridhyashram attaching my neighbouring plots for keeping common Roof of G+3 Floors where various health care services can be provided and ground floor for clinic, garage for medical Van, offices etc. I have submitted my proposal in Bengali language to one of our earlier LCS who is presently working in KMC Building Department, expecting his influence will get me to attach the neighbouring plots and one builder jointly with me to construct the Bridhyashram. Whenever I meet him and enquire about the progress, he expresses his extreme busy schedule for party's work and meetings. His father and I were having very good relation and he was very sincere and hard worker for the **CPM Party** but starved for survival. We both are APL/BPL category and somehow managing with mere income from service/pension. Next, I have again given that Proposal to Secretary of M/s…… Club in our Block where majority is the **CPM Party's** supporter. Generally, every Block one Club has been established where members are busy throughout the year conducting various cultural programmes, all God/Goddess's Puja celebration by public subscription and Business people's contributions. Any construction in the Block the members will come forward for collecting there share for smooth construction. Political leaders are indulging them to capture the total vote from the Block. Likewise our standing MP, Sri …. contributed Rupees Four Lakh from his MP Fund of wards/Blocks development.

As per **'SB's** observation **this contribution is nothing but making white money from black money. Why Government will contribute such a huge amount to Clubs when such Associations are earning lakhs of Rupees per annum. In Audit why there is no Report for this faulty expenditures.** This club used to put the Banner of this MP's contribution on the outside of Club Room before the present Government's took over. This Club has managed one Plot by force and constructed one Auditorium with open space for all cultural activities. Next, another Plot this club has captured by force on south side of the …….. Road attached with our own Plot and one Sri ………. and family's Plot where our 1.1/2 Cottahs of land submerged with one small pond. This land belongs to one land owner who is living nearby and given to one Builder/ Promoter for construction in the year 2005 taking help from Police Force. Immediately this Club arranged 150 to 200 women Force for stopping the construction works reason they are performing all Gods/Goddesses Puja celebration whereas this Club has got own Auditorium with open space nearby Club Premises. This I have come to know from one Builder. In the captioned Book, it is well defined, who are these Gods/ Goddesses. They are highly spiritual Human Beings born in the society to eradicate all evils thinking of human mind to restore humanity in the society in those days when people were living like a slave cornered with untouchability. Nevertheless, our CPM Party's self-centered power crazy leaders have accepted this social evils thinking and indulged these evils thinking people to capture the vote. They have forgotten the teachings of Marxism philosophy. I am enclosing herewith my Proposal in Bengali languages for your kind perusal. Therefore, I would request you to be kind enough to help me to construct the proposed **Bridhyashram** and to start various activities for senior citizens through my registered **NGO...............**

During the reign of your 34 years ruling you have made such a strong **Burgeon Platform** for the benefit of **20% Burgeon People** through all bureaucrats, creating various Units/Unions in Educational Institutions, Industrial and in Business Circles, DYFI, and Women Associations, Clubs etc. for continuing your Anarchism/Nepotism through Slogan, Procession to keep alive your Self-Centered Power Crazy Dynasty, which will only look after Industrialists, Business Communities, your own Kings, Leaders, Cadres etc. to make them Billionaires/Millionaires. For fulfilling this achievement you have left lakhs of crores liabilities for next Government to clear with unbearable hardship.

Yours truly,

Laxmi Nayaran

**Honourable Chief Minister of West Bengal**
**Department of Chief Minister's Office,**
**Government of West Bengal,**
**Writer's Buildings, First Floor, F Block,**
**Kolkata – 700001**

**Respected Sir/Madam,**

## SUB: MAA, MATI & MANUSH IN REVISED SIXTH EDITION OF MY BOOK –"EVOLUTION OF HUMAN BEINGS AND SOCIETY"

This is with reference to my earlier letter dated ........... enclosing therewith various letters and documents regarding Kolkata Municipal Corporation's malafide activities and negative responds of my request for construction of **Bridhyashram (Old-Age-Home) as per our NGO- "Purbachal Senior Citizens, Society"'s Proposals** in Bengali, copy attached herewith. Also attaching herewith a copy of letter addressed to **General Secretary of West Bengal Communist Party of India, 31, Alimuddin Street, Kolkata-700019** as per sample letter (Revised) from the captioned Book mentioned above including some Foot Note (N.B.) below in the last page. As per **SB's** observation and notification to you and to the Commissioners of Kolkata Municipal Corporation in time-to-time **SB** now has confirmed that sitting on the **Burgeon ruling Platform** of **20% People** to establish **MAA, MATI & MANUSH** Society of **80% APL & BPL Categories People** is going to be a **vague slogan.** In addition, to make Kolkata same as London is simply to build a **Castle in the Air**. Elaborate details are given below:

**KMC Act** has been established in the year 1876 by British Ruler to collect taxes from Indians as per their will and wish.

Current rules and methodology as per the decision of present Autonomous Body for fulfilling the Political Parties requirements. Now they are advertising that they are following E'Governance system by which consumers can get all details in Web Site. This Web Site is only for making payments through internet. E'Governance system should clarify entire KMC Rules and regulations of all activities through all media channels, Internet, Newspaper, and Mobile. In addition, customer care services for enquiring everything in person or by mobile. There should not be any **Hearing Cell** for mutation and other matters for negotiations and adjustments attended by Agents and/or by self- attendant for making extra money.

To accomplish the above remodeling of **Kolkata City (City of Joy)** in compare with the **London City** we must seek 100% finance from Central Government inviting International Renowned Builder/Contractor as per detailed analysis, a separate Sheets attached with the letter to the present Prime Minister of India with 9th Edition Book.

As per **SB's** observation and notification, in **Burgeon ruling Platform of 20% People's Government** cannot make any development in the City due to deadly corruption of 99% Leaders, Cadres and Workers have forced **80% people** to become **Revenue Cancer Patient. Honesty is the crime in the present Society.** Because of this reason Government assigning all development works to KMC so that all the executives after distribution of their own share some percentage can be put to the Government treasury Department. A simple example was **Trident Lamp Project**. When there will be great noise in public and with media, Government will not give such things to CBI. In the Captioned Book **SB** proposed for fly over for public and for vehicles. These are the few achievements through KMC in two years, which will never come to the public notice. What **SB** proposed in the captioned Book for development for Jadavpur Constituency Area but during the two years unaccounted sources of income accumulated but development same as where it was. Being a **Secretary** of **NGO-........................... Society"** I did send one letter dated ........... 2013 to Shri .............. along with the above mentioned Proposal for **Bridhyashram (old-Age-Home)** and blank copy of Minutes of Meeting. **Sri ..............** is not giving clearance to **Sri ............, Executive Member of the ...........  Club and also In-charge of TMC of our Block No........** Sri ....... has confirmed that he has already taken consent of my neighbouring 7Plot Owners, totaling to Four Bighas of land and agreed to give the contract to construct the **Bidhyashram** from **Promoters' Allocation**. Being the Promoters, we can make the development in the Block as per commitment given in the Proposal without taking any financial help from Government. Kindly advise Sri ............ to give the clearance to Sri............... who will be busy for Panchayat Election upto 9 July'13.

As per your kind and sympathetic action in responds to my earlier requests I have received one letter on ........... from Department of Chief Minister's Office signed by Secretary and Joint Secretary to the Chief Minister addressed to the Commissioner of Kolkata Municipal Corporation and copy to me. Under signed did send a reply on ............ to the Joint Secretary and copy to the **Commissioner of KMC**. Both the letters' copy attached herewith. On ........, undersigned met **Joint Commissioner, Sri ..........** who advised me to come on Wednesday after discussing with **CM(R), Sri.........** to finalise

my two appeals for reducing my two plots tax dispute as per last years bill and **NOC for Bridhyashram**. In this matter I understand from their discussion that there was tremendous pressure from the Government to increase the revenue and accordingly the Axe has been thrown to my case and **CM (R).** always threaten to send my case to Tribunal. This is another thrashing to the **MAA, MATI & MANUSH Slogan by the 20% Burgeon.**

My another Appeal for **Bridhyashram** in Bhadreswar, Hooghly to the Joint Secretary against the Criminal Case for Cheater, Sri ............ First hearing of he said Case will appear on ......... supported by **Sri ..........** who will prearrange with PP to argue in favour of the said Cheater to disqualify all of my claim agreed and signed by the Cheater. Kindly advise Joint Secretary to help me to recover my money to be utilized for Senior Citizens of that locality. All details about the status of the land given to him.

Thanking you for your kind and sympathetic consideration.

Yours truly,

# Part - III

Honourable Prime Minister of India,
Prime Minister's House,
7 Race Course Road,
New Delhi -110001

Respected Sir,

## SUB: MONKI BAATH OF 80% BPL & APL CATEGORIES OF PEOPLE RULED BY 20% BURGEON PEOPLE THROUGH THE GOVERNMENT'S NEPOTISM, ANARCHISM AND AUTOCRATIC ADMINASTRATION

## REF: NINTH EDITION- "EVOLUTION OF HUMAN BEINGS AND SOCIETY"

This is in continuation of earlier letter dated ......... 2014 attaching **8th Edition Book** mentioned below and amended in this Captioned Book. Presently the Government is earning few lakhs crores of rupees by seizing few hundred banks' accounts of non-member companies registered under Companies Act through Ministry of Incorporation Affairs. For the Last three years Government could not make **Investors' Protection Act** and having absolute power why Government is not taking over all those companies for running and/or attaching their Properties for auction and refunding all investors' money and paying all employees' outstanding salaries of those companies. Banks have reduced FD annual Rate and subsequently increased various charges to keep their present profit margin. Please think now how much return all those **80% APL & BPL Categories of people** will get keeping their savings in the Banks. Government is making various developments in all sectors and planning to make some Smart City, like-wise High Speed Bullet-Proof Railway lines and trains. Government's Development activities in all Sectors increasing Income/Profit of **20% Burgeon People** and Cost of Development by increasing Rate of Products, Taxes, Cess, Duties, reducing Bank's FD interest Rate and increasing their various charges in all Accounts is effect very badly to all **80% BPL AND APL Categories of People** whose Income will never increase. More over the present Government is trying to reduce rate of PF Pension which mostly from **Senior Citizens of 80% BPL AND APL Categories of Peoples'** deposits deducted from their remunerations when they all were working in Private and/or Government's Organisations and presently their Pension of September 2015 is still pending and not credited in their Bank about 3 to 4 months. And even after clearing all deficiency due pension will be credited after one month on receipt of getting return benefit statement from Share Market of all EPF deposits which are invested. Government should think that any development for any Sector **20% Burgeon People** will get the benefit and increase of product rates, taxes, duties etc. will be burden for **80% APL & BPL Categories of people** and they will become poor and poorer. Ultimately they have to change their profession for their lovely hood by looting, robbery, killing, terrorizing people etc. **Human resources are the main Assets of the Country.** They invent and discover all new things from this earth. To utilize them **100% we have to give them 100% Education, 100% Employment and 100% Health.** Central Autocratic Government presently occupied by **Profit motivated 20% Burgeon People and Business Communities' Societies** as per **Swamy Vivekananda's** 3rd stages Classes of Societies which narrated in the Captioned Book. **Central Autocratic Government** given Power to **SEBI** most corrupted unit in the Share Market (details are given in Captioned Book) occupied by **'A' Group of Companies** dominated by **Reliance Group of Companies**, capturing few hundred Non-Member of Companies and seizing their all Bank accounts. A**s per Economic Theory defines Value of money lies in Circulation of Money** and Government is earning few lakhs crores in a year through all banks for making **Crores of 80% BPL AND APL Categories of People poor and poorer.** Central Government's introduction of **Aadhar Cards** nothing but to remove **Statistical Data of APL & BPL Ration Cards** which will give **Status of 80% BPL AND APL Categories of People.** As per latest **TOI's** report Government is further planning to increase all **MP's Remuneration** which Once done in earlier Government's Dynasty. Peoples humble prayer to you on behalf of all Senior Citizens of **80% BPL AND APL Categories of People** to be kind enough to get released all of their deposit amounts including monthly outstanding **MIS.** Few lakh Peoples have become worst sufferer for not getting their MIS and matured Investment Amount deposited with the three companies, namely - **a) M/s Rose Valley Chain Marketing Systems Ltd., b) M/s LRN Finance Ltd. and c) Kolkata Weir Industries Ltd.** whose detailed analysis sheets are attached for your kind perusal.

As per the previous letter of dated 10.12.2014 wherein given details of various **20% Burgeon peoples (at the end)** those who are actually ruling the **80% APL & BPL Categories of people** and becoming millionaire and billionaire through their **Elected Power Crazy Representatives.** They are spending hard cash for all elected representatives on election period.

## PREVIOUS LETTER FOR ALL POLITICAL PARTIES WHOM SO <u>EVER IT MAY CONCERN REVISED IN THE CAPTIONED BOOK</u>

## SUB: EIGHTH EDITION OF MY BOOK – <u>"EVOLUTION OF HUMAN BEINGS AND SOCIETY"</u>

The British Ruler did hand over the reign of this country, India, to one of their pet Indian family members in Democratic Platform advising to rule the country as per their established law and Divide & Rule policy and keeping alive all casteism, religious fundamentalism etc. Therefore, the generation to generation his predecessors can rule the country. Accordingly, numbers of Rulers/Kings have increased from Single to Thousands to Lakhs in three Categories, as **Administrative,**

**Financial and Judiciary**. They have made **Burgeon ruling Platform** of **20% Burgeon People** ruling over **80% APL & BPL categories of people** in the **Federal System** of Democratic Country. Our Society is **paternal system of Society** since beginning when Society formed. In the captioned Books **SB** suggested there should be only **two Reservation 50% for Women and 50% for OBC (includes all castes, all religions, all sexes etc.). But priority will be 70% son of the soil and 30% for all others and 100% for all meritorious A Grade with 90% and above.** But in this democratic country every Castes/ Religions etc. demanding for separate Reservation Percentage.

In Hinduism, there are four **Yugas** such as **Satya, Treta**, **Drapad**, and Ca**li Yuga** presently running. **Man-Pita (Father)** is the head of the family. Man is dominating in the family as well as in the Society. Women populations are increasing and they are capable of managing the entire Society in much better way than men if they are not **Self Centered Power Crazy Women**. Factually, Woman is much more superior to Male Person. First, Woman is the creator of **Human Beings.** Man deposits seeds and Woman preserves the seeds feed them and bring them in the Society after 8 or 9 months. Woman is much sexier than Male Person, but Woman has controlling element i.e. **Diffidence/(Lajja)/Shyness** which controls the sex of Woman. Sex is natural requirement and demand. As per **Unani and Ayurvedic's** explanation woman body's has eight places filling of Sex sensation on touch. However, man has got only in two places. In the '**Quran'**, Dress Code for Woman specified for complete body **cover** with **Veil (Borkha).** Now the modern Society's Woman prefers to expose their body for beautification, competition in Fashion Parade and elsewhere.

In the Captioned Book **SB (Sukumar Banerjee),** Speaker of this **Book** suggested for **Self-Government** systems from **Block level to District level**. To implement the said systems Government has to pass Bill for taking control of all Clubs, Temples, Mosques, Churches and other religious Centers under Government control and to set up one **BDO Office** for administering the **Block** for developing the followings:

All unemployed people as per Mobile Employment Exchange Record in the Block should get job. In all religious Centers, all devotees should come as usual to pray almighty as per individual's religious belief in their respective temples, Mosques, Churches and any other respective Centers after depositing their contributions, any articles etc to the **Block Office**. **Block Offices** employed attendants attached to temples, Mosques, Churches and other religious Centers will accompany them to the Worship Place. All Priests, Pandas, Imams, Moulabis, Fathers and other Religious Heads will get remuneration every month from the Devotees' contributions and other valuables from the **Block Office**. All unemployed **Club** members will get job as Security Man or as per their Skilled/Unskilled capability. Total Income from **Club** activities will be under control of **BDO Office**. Self-Employed Individuals in any business and/or any Professions should register their working details in **BDO Office** to contribute certain percentage from their Income for Block Developments such as **100% Education, Health, Cultural activities etc.** No Cadres of any Political Parties are required to visit to any Business and Professionals' Offices to collect the Funds for their Political Parties requirements for paying salary to their cadres only and maintaining all expenses for parties' propaganda, vague slogan etc. instead all unemployed will get their respective jobs in their Block through **BDO Office.** Political Parties funds requirements are the main cause of corruptions in entire Bureaucratic systems. All political Parties' leaders have interlinked relations in the corruption. They abuse stating '**Dishonest**' to each other but cannot go further for fear of getting gluey mud in their character. There is no ambiguity that most of the leaders are suffering from **Revenue Cancer** and no chance of getting cure because their Billion/Trillion Dollars in foreign Banks will remain unclaimed. What a pity and shameful matters for us.

Now to cure all the **Revenue Cancer patients** we have to establish **MAA, MATI & MANUSH Society.** First think for **MAA-(Bharat MAA)** for whom we have to change the political structure i.e. Federal Systems to Presidential Systems elected by the people, of the people and for the people. Next to, choose Leader for President, who thinks for people from '**MATI', (Block to District label).** Next to, choose '**MANUSH' (Man or Woman)** and for this, we have to go to Hinduism Story of **Treta Yuga**, when **Ram** worshiped for arrival of '**MAA' "Dur**ga" to kill '**Ravana'.** We can choose from only Woman, who is superior to Man, but does not possess any **Self-Centered Power Crazy Mentality** except developing Ego and direct Injection to all **Revenue Cancer Patients** to establish **"MAA, MATI & MANUSH Society".** Any Leader from any State if claim that he is only eligible for becoming competent Head of the Country by showing his only Industrial growth which benefitted only **20% Burgeon**

**People** not for **80% of APL & BPL categories of people. SB's** question that by Industrial growth can he prove **100% employed in the State, 100% Education, Health and 100% secured life?**

Now '**SB**' is going to analyse religious fundamentalism and some idea to remove inhuman treatment by Fundamentalist through the **Self-Government System** already explained in the foregoing method in the **Captioned Book**.

1. <u>**Fundamentalism in Hinduism:**</u>

In Hinduism, there were **33 Crores Spiritual Persons as Gods and Goddesses** arrived to remove inhuman treatment by Fundamentalist to establish peace and humanity in the Society. Out of them, there are Supreme Spiritual Persons-Gods arrived in four different **Yuga (Period)** like **Sri Bishnu/ Brahma/ Shiva in Satya Yuga, Sri Ram in Treta Yuga, Sri Krishna in Drapad Yuga and in Cali Yuga:-Sri Budhya Deb, Sri Jaganath, Sri Chaitanya Mahaprabhu, Sri Ramakrishna, Sri Pareshnath/Tirthankara Sri Guru Nanak etc.**

Some **Spiritual Persons/Gods** created some powerful Gods and Goddesses through sexual activities. As an Example **Sri Shiva, God** who was the **King** of **Kailash Parbat** and throughout the years and years was on **Yoga/Sadhana** of Soul. And become so powerful strong **Person-God** that **He** could transfer his power to **Ravana** who was worshiping **Sri Shiva** later on made that **Sri Shiva** his captive and whenever, **Ravana** moving for conquer, he used to carry **Sri Shiva** on his shoulder. However, **Sri Shiva** told to **Ravana** that if he keeps **Sri Shiva** for any reason on the land he would not be able to pull him out from that place. **Ravana** was under tremendous urinal pressure and he has to keep him on **Deoghar Land**, now in Jharkhand State, is the First **Shiva Temple** in India.

There is another story about the **Stone Image of Sri Shiva.** 'MAA-Pārbati' wife of Sri Shiva, was daughter of **Janak**, Maharaja of Himalaya. 'MAA- Pārbati' was worshiping **Sri Shiva. O**ne day, when she was in the **Kailash Sarobar** with her friends for taking bath, **Sri Shiva** nearby was in inanimate condition in **Yoga/Sadhana** on one mountain. **Sri Shiva** suddenly got wake up when some women were taking bath with high volume sounding games. **Sri Shiva's** Sex excitement awakened his penis, which he extended long towards those women, and those who were looking to the long penis started loud utterance expressing joy but **MAA-Pārbati** inserted that Penis in her Bush. Latter on **MAA-Pārbati's** friend groups cut that Penis. The first **Image of Sri Shiva** in **Deoghar Temple** is in the shape of **Cut Penis** inserted in the **Bush of MAA-Pārbati.** Throughout the country on **Shiva Day,** people are worshiping this image sacredly so that they get same power like **Sri Shiva.** Now **SB's** queries why religious fundamentalists should kill **Mahatma Gandhi**, who arrived in this country as **God** to establish Humanity with secularity without violence. And, why world famous painter, **M. F. Husain** has to leave his country for not doing any crime but for making his own thinkable Goddess's Image. It is wrong **Fatwa** when we can worship the Image of our **Shiva-God Image and/or Stone made Image.**

Laxmi Nayaran

1. <u>**Muslim's Islamic Religion in 'Quran' & Christian Religion in 'Bible'**</u>

2. Both the religions are accepted by each very friendly. Moreover, both the Religions are merciful and they believe, God will punish them for their crime. Now in India also Religious harmony extended in marital relation with each other Love. Moreover, India is a Secular, Democratic Country. **God, Christ** direct from **Mother Marry,** sacrificed himself for the cause of peace and humanity. **Prophet, Hazarat Muhammad**, illiterate, cannot read and write anything but Angel, messenger of **Allah (Almighty)**, bestowed **Allah's Prophecy** through **Prophet's** versions in '**Quran**'. In **Quran**, there is no direct punishment announced like **'Fatwa'** to any one for any crime but left on **Allah** who will decide. We should not encourage any Fundamentalists' Group to create terrorism in the Society creating inhuman crimes. **SB** feels all-religious Heads-Pundits', Gurus, Imams, Moulabis, and Fathers; jointly conduct one Convention to instigate/inspire to all religious people to conduct prayer everyday to strengthen their brainpower and to gain the following benefits of **Health and Mind**:

1. Improve 'Immune Function'
2. Reduce risk of death from heart attack and stroke
3. Reduce stress and increased peace of mind
4. Reduction and Elimination of panic attacks, anxiety and depression
5. Reduce impacts from chronic pain
6. A more positive, happy out-look on 'Life'
7. A healthier, longer, more fulfilled 'Life'

In addition, of above prayers we should invite them to attend Temples, Gurdwaras, Churches, Mosques and other any religious Places on various occasions announcing any auspicious Day celebration through broadcasting channels. For all these we should insist Government to take over all the Religious Places and set up one **BDO office** to manage the situation. By this, Income will increase and everybody will get good job so that idle brain will not choose any criminal jobs.

In view of the above **SB** feels that the **'Fatwa'** announced for **Writers-Taslima Nasrin & Salman Rushdie** can be withdrawn. **SB** feels that if Government passes the Bill for taking over all the Clubs, Religious Places can remove all Terrorists set-ups moving door to door from **Block label to District label** by giving them employment through Mobile Employment Exchange and Broad Casting Media Channel for over all development of **80% BPL and APL categories of people** then **'MAA. MATI & MANUSH' Society** is established. Once the above Society is established then unlimited democratic rights of **20% Burgeon Peoples** can be synchronized for stopping their **Nepotism and Anarchism** in the Society over **80% BPL and APL Categories of people.**

As per Swami Vivekananda, Casteism originated from division of labours details of which are given in the captioned **Book:-**

A) First The Tasks of **Saints/Father/Brahmins/Gurus/ Moulabis'** to impart **Gnayana (knowledge)** to all and then became the Ruler of the Society in **Satya Yuga.**

B) Second The Tasks of **Khatryas/Warriors** whose works are to protect the Country and all human beings from enemies and then became the **Ruler/King** of the Society in **Treta Yuga and Drapad Yuga.**

C) Third The Tasks of **Baishya/Bania/Businessmen** who is providing all commodities and services to all human beings by **Barter System and/or by Cash** and then started controlling the entire economy and became the Ruler of the Society in **Cali Yuga**.

D) **Sudras/Workers** are the ones who perform all various works like cleanliness and other various activities/works for all human beings in the society. These **Sudras/Workers** are becoming poor and poorer; they may revolt for making **'Proletariat Dictatorship'** to rule the Society. **All these four divisions of labours are categorized as 'Caste'.**

Presently in the **Burgeon Ruling Platform,** your unlimited democratic rights for **20% Burgeon people** ruling over **80% APL & BPL Categories of people** cannot control **Price Index.** In the present **Burgeon Ruling Platform 99%** people are vitiated to earn extra money by cheating, coercion, false representation etc. Everybody wants to become business man. Now nobody wants to work on piece rate. All technicians want to work on contract basis. Latest **TOI'S** report one Electrician is earning more than one Engineer. Like was all Service men/ Professionals are looting money by all means especially there are new business categories like Commission Agents, Media etc. who can overturn the Dynasty propagating false slogans, false statistical reports financed by **A Group of Companies**. In the **Captioned Book, SB** suggested in the **Price Index Chapter** profit margin 3 to 4 times in **MRP Price** on factory rate should be reduced and fresh cultivated products in retail markets every handling, charging more than 100% to 200% profits should be reduced after addition of transportation charges only. In the **Shopping Mall**, retail-prices are more than in the open retail market price. Moreover, in **Whole Sale Mall** fresh cultivated products rates are more than **Open Retail Market**. **SB** strongly condemned Emergency Food Bill for poor people in earlier Dynasty. This is another deception to the **80% BPL & APL Categories of people.** You are well aware that your **Fair Price Shop** is very much-corrupted unit in the Society. This is only for Government's own Party dominated States for election campaign and those people benefitted will earn extra money by selling in the market on high rate. In addition, your distribution bureaucratic system is dangerously corrupted unit in the **Burgeon Ruling Platform.** We are Second Largest Populated Country in the World. You are trying to implement all systems of World Kings whose population is $1/3^{rd}$ of our Population. Implementation of all Financial Expertise rewarded in the country of World King will boost up status of **20% Burgeon Peopl**e to increase corruption, terrorism etc. in the Democratic Country.

In the Captioned Book suggested 100% employment by implementing **Self Government Systems in Gram Panchayat and in the City**. For this, we have to arrange **National Religious Convention** to support **Emergency Bill** for controlling all States' **Religious Associations/ Institutions** and all **Clubs' Sports and Cultural activities'** development under guideline of Central Government. For this, we have to establish **States' Sena** to visit door to door along with **BDO Officer** for preparing Bio-Data of every member of the house for their development.

### 3. <u>Money Market/Share Market:</u>

This Market is only for **20% Burgeon peoples' interest.** In addition, your full-hearted endeavours to boost up their interest you are after **FDI** Investment for higher Percentage of **NAV** in Share Market for selling the shares on higher rate to make them Billionaire. By this system, **80% APL & BPL categories of peoples'** are in calamitous condition and is deteriorating as per details given below:

Share Market under control of **SEBI** which is again under control of **'A' Group of companies'** leadership for manipulating under guideline of **Reliance Group, Financial King of our Country.** This King is continuously satisfying The Government's Kings, all Bureaucrats, Ministers, etc. through all **'A' Group of companies** by giving their own shares at lowest price so that the same shares can be sold in Boom period. In exchange, they are dictating the Government to pass the Bill for extra ordinary power to **SEBI**. So that **SEBI** can interfere in all other non-member companies' business affairs registered under Companies Act with Incorporation Certificate from Ministry of Corporate Affairs including authority to collect money from public against deposit Certificate, Debenture Certificate and Redeemable Preference Share Certificate when **FDI** investment is not responding. Very recently present Government announced entire systems in Government offices will be under Internet Systems for which reliance group of companies will contribute Five Lakh Crores of rupees. Possibly in exchange Government may give them relief from paying Royalty for extracting petroleum Raw Materials drilling from **KG D6 Field** and there is no movement of collecting huge last year outstanding of Royalty in present time. If you remember during 1994 Chairman of **UTI** made a deal with Reliance Group to crash down the **US-64 M.F. Scheme** in exchange of receiving Reliance share @Rs.1/- for his own shares when we **all 80% of BPL & APL categories people** were getting **26% dividend** per annum. Finally, that scheme is now closed. Earlier Government has put huge unpaid outstanding **EPF** deposit in Share Market and possibly entire **EPF** deposit of all salaried personnel also will be invested in Share Market by opening an individual Bank A/c where dividend/profit will be credited to all Individual A/c. But as per **SB's** experience Brokers of all **'A' Group of companies** through their strong manipulation will crash down **NAV** rate and nothing will add in the Individual A/c for indefinite Bull period. **As per SB's opinion that EPF entire amount should be kept in Mutual Fund under Debt Scheme so that some amount will be credited in Individual A/c.** Your earlier Finance Ministry as per last year's News Paper Report there was one white paper came out for **2G Scam** and other various Scams linked with the same Finance Minister's name, which with craftiness method the matter got clean chit. This Ministry's I.T. Department under the table clearing all disputes every day. In one case being Nil Return Holder forgot to claim his TDS refund but with the help of subordinate with I.T.O.'s approval, that man got his refund as per Credit shows in the Book of his Pan Number Account as per normal procedure by giving cash 10% to 15%. Another Case of one Advocate who was torturing another man for huge undue cash receipt who has given one detailed letter to **C.I.T**. enforcement Department for the said Advocate whose yearly Income nearly to Rs. Fifty Lakhs. and same man written one letter dated ............ 2013 to earlier Government for Attn Prime Minister to pass the **Emergency Bill** for collecting Infrastructure Tax on Profit/ Income quarterly from the following **Burgeon People @5% on Rupees 5 lakhs to 10 lakhs, 10% on over 10 lakhs to 50 Lakhs, 15% on over 50 Lakhs to 10 Crores and 20% over 10 Crores and above.**

1. All Bureaucrats **(IAS, IPS, IFS, ETC.)**
2. All Professionals **(All Judicial Members, Doctors, Engineers etc.** those who earn maximum in Cash)
3. All Business communities **(Commission Agents, Media, Shop Keepers, Hospitals, Hotels, Educational Institutions etc. They are earning maximum in Cash.**

All Industrialists; These extraordinary Brain and Money Power Peoples building Industries for producing all machineries, commodities for meeting all human needs should demand profitable Price for development and increase of Industries. But Government's demand/requirement of extra money these Industrialists have to increase the Price which becomes burden for **80% BPL & APL Categories of People.**

All Political Leaders/Ministers-Kings; Elected by the People, for the People, of the People but almost **90% are Self-Motivated Power Crazy Anti National Kings, more of them insist for Cash.** Above collection will help **80% BPL & APL of categories of People** to get **100% Education, 100% employment and 100% Health Care** to maintain the internal peace and security in the whole nation from extortion, terrorism, separatism, communalism/ fundamentalism, corruption etc. These also will make improvement of national feeling and disciplined culture by curing all **Revenue Cancer Patients from Burgeon People**. **80% BPL & APL Categories of People** are under impression that Judicial Sector is independent judgment and law making Authority but as per Indian Constitution they are on the horns of a dilemma. Factually Elected Peoples' Representatives are the Supreme King for settling all investors' fate. And it is evident that the Supreme Kings are busy for making lakhs of crores from investors' investments with so called seized all Ponji companies for the benefit of the **20% Burgeon People. Supreme Kings** can instruct all **Judicial Heads** to pass an Order for attachment for taking over Scheduled properties of all Ponji companies for refunding Investors' total outstanding money. **SB** one of the worst victims being a founder member of the registered non profitable **NGO** for construction of **Bridhyashram** for poor senior citizens among **80% BPL & APL Categories of People. SB** has driven from pillar to post in this state (i.e. Appeal to Ministry, KMC, all Judicial Courts, and Enforcement Directorate, everywhere reply is they cannot assure any definite time/period and result). **SB** attached the following letters for your kind perusal:-

1. Copy of letter dated ......... 2015 to the Chairman, Security Exchange Board of India, Regional Office, L & T Chambers, Kamac Street, Kolkata-700020.

2. Copy of letter the dated ........ 2015 to the Special Director of Enforcement, CGO Complex, DF Block, MSO Buildng, A-Wing, 6th Floor, Kolkata-700064

3. Copy of letter dated........... 2015 addressed to the Addl. Commissioner and Joint Commissioner of Police (Crime), 18, Lal Bajar Police Station (Head Quarter), Kolkata-700001

4. Annexure-A/1- Detailed Analysis Sheet of above mentioned three companies along with latest outstanding due amount up to ........... 2015.

## ANNEXURE-A/2 OF PRIMINISTER' LETTER

Considering similarity of **London City's** Geographical and environmental equation **'SB'** suggested remodeling of **Kolkata City** should give special Priority as per elaborate detailed separate statement attached. But before remodeling Government should abolish **Calcutta Municipal Corporation Act** established in the year **1876 by British Ruler** having absolute Bureaucratic Power of independent Parallel Government Administratively, Financially and Judicially having only one member, **Elected Mayor** from state government. Most corrupted Organisation in the Country.

## Road construction, cleaning, Sewage system, maintenance etc.

### A) Road Construction:-

Road should be eclipse type i.e. from middle with little high sloping to both side by asphalt mixtures and after roller application of sufficient extra thick Coal Tar should be applied so that water stagnant will not be there and stone chips will not come out when vehicles are running on the Road in the rainy season. For maintenance, there should be permanent maintenance Workshop in every Constituency and all employed technicians will conduct the maintenance works instead of contractors who are the main source to manage huge amount of extra cash money. All political cadres/workers required to be employed in the Block level to supervise the every maintenance works in the Block.

### B) Drainage, Cleaning, and Sewage system:-

All open drainages should be shield by 100" dia or more, concrete CS Pipes with rubber lining or alternatively both side end of the drainage should be concrete shield with little height from the both Road and then build up new shopping mall on the shield area to shift all city hawkers /temporary shopkeepers from pavement. The same 100" dia concrete CS Pipes would be laid in the depth sea to the extent of few kilometers away. Entire drainage water and sewage system would be pumped out to the sea through the concrete CS Pipe Line. There should be both side drainage systems on the Road. Road cleaning would be done by water hosepipe attaching with the river water pipe line Tap installed on the roadside early in the morning. There should be HDP made garbage storage Box installed on the every Electric Light Post where the people will put all their home garbage packet. Garbage Van will come to collect garbage from the storage Box. All employed Cadres/Workers should be alert to stop unloading all civil materials on the Roadside.

C) **Drinking Water**:

All employed Cadres/Workers should check all the damaged Taps/Valves where continuous wastage of water flowing. After repairing Cadres/workers should arrange waterline inside the hutment/Flat so that those people need not put queue on the Roadside for collecting drinking water.

D) **Slum Dwellers**:

To remove slum dwellers/hawkers from both side of the Railway Line running through City, we should cover the Line by constructing multi-storied building for shopkeepers and slum dwellers.

E) **International standard Multi-Storied Inter-State Bus Terminus from Esplanade to Babu Ghat Area:-**

This Terminus will have the following facilities:

i) **Basement:** Local city buses & Inter-State Buses along with

    a)   Petrol Pumps & small maintenance Workshop,

b) Various Fast-Food Canteens,

c) Medical Shops & Clinics and

d) Gift Articles Shops.

ii) **Ground Floor:**

a) **Side Corner** for Reserve Buses, Car Parking, & Fast-Food Canteens

b) **Middle Portion** reserved for Seminars, Political-Parties Meetings and for any celebrations on chargeable basis for all. If Government can arrange its own **TV Channel** then all sorts of publicity, announcements can stop all processions and Slogans.

iii) **First Floor & Second Floor: B**oth for Shopping Mall for bringing all **C**entral Kolkata's Hawkers and temporary shopkeepers.

F) **Ganga River:**

a) To make few bridges from Barackpore to Diamond Harbour for interlink Metro rail across River in Western Side.

b) Below the bridges there will be Station for High Speed small AC/Non AC double Decker Steamer with Canteen and Bath/WC facility to be launched from Barackpore to Diamond Harbour.

Laxmi Nayaran

**Honourable Prime Minister of India,**
**Prime Minister's House,**
**3, Race Course Road,**
**New Delhi**

Respected Sir,

## SUB: REVISED FIFTH EDITION OF MY BOOK -
## "EVOLUTION OF HUMAN BEINGS AND SOCIETY"

First, I express my sincere congratulation to you for your receiving best honour from United States of America for giving relief from their economic depression by utilizing your financial expertise, which I have learned from **T.O.I.** newspaper few months before. For our country where 80% people are living in Villageand 20% in City and where 99% people are vitiated under control of self centered power crazy dirty politicians. As per **SB's** suggestion, I most humbly feel that there should be new elected Leader without any political parties' nomination and taking Bond from them for honest services yearly basis from Block level to District level. I am sure it will bring out spectacular changes amongst the people. I would request your honour to refer this Book, Chapter..., on **Price Index.** By local self-government systems we can set up agricultural based Small Scale Industries and job oriented business development if our Government adopts **Micro Finance System** of Noble laureate **Dr. Mohd. Yunus** and we can create jobs for village people to abstain from rushing to city. It is deception in disguise to the village poor people providing 100 days jobs, which cannot give total relief for survival. Your globalization and liaise-fare system without control has made all business communities in a pull to become billionaire very fast. All mall owners have captured and/or taken all cultivated lands and fruit gardens/ farms on lease to make the supply market under their control for earning maximum profit, result of which the price of food products is running so high and the government control has become in a jeopardized osition.

I am inclined to think that the local self-government system, which this Book has suggested from pages..... to ........., may induce the people not to press their demand for separate Statehood and terrorizing people to acquire power to rule the society.

Introduction of local self-government system may work as a great 'Mantra' for bringing out much needed change by removing above mentioned evil thinking and activities in the society. Consider my further appeal to the Government that the emergency services listed in this Book, may kindly be considered as most priority sector for declaring ordinances to cease democratic right of unionism for stopping the work for any reason. Moreover, this ordinance may support industrial and economical growth constantly. Educational Institution also may kindly be included in that list.

Most disturbing elements for economical growth in this country is religious fundamentalism which created horror, terrorism etc. among the people of one religion to other religion. If we refer this Book, page from.... to.... we can learn that religion established in the society by the people, for the people and of the people to live in peace with humanity. When people of society become in unrest position then one spiritual person took birth in the society as God, Allah and Bhagawan to eradicate the unrest position and restore the society in peace with humanity. God lives in the heart/soul of Human Beings not in the air. We can see the God in any Form through our heart/soul, which enlighten through meditation, dhyana, worshiping etc. The Custodians/Authorities of all religions are changing the application methods and are creating superstition forcefully among the people like opium to rule the society with horror and terrorism. We must influence intellectuals/educationists to write a book on religion to educate people in the Educational Institution.

Religious fundamentalism divided our country in Three Part. Now we should try to unite them considering similar culture and languages with absolute autonomy as individual statehood status and local self-government system from Block level to District level. However, sovereignty will remain with United India represented by people representative from all states. By this, we can restrain the expansionist, China who started capturing our land from Ladakh to Arunachal Pradesh declaring, advertising as its or their own land after conquering Tibet. China got independence after our independence from British Ruler and today China's economical growth is roaring so high that all developed countries economy will be under its control and their per capita income now has become more than double than India after 1981.

Now it is alarming that foreign aid to rebellions and terrorists in our country may bring the civil war to make China and Pakistan joint attack to capture our entire North and North East area very soon. We must bring back national feeling among all people to protect the country's sovereignty.

Another blunder we have done by investing our public deposit in Provident Fund in the share market, result of which monthly P.F. Pension to the Senior Citizen remain outstanding for two months at the end of the month.

At the end **SB** has challenged if we do not bring new Act and/or include punishment in Lokpal Bill to remove corruption in entire bureaucratic system, i.e. in Administration, Finance, Judicial and Defense everywhere created through democracy of Political Parties for achieving power financed by Business Communities for spending crores of rupees in **Procession, Slogan, and Gathering etc** and for paying few listeners/ attendance to make the gatherings in few lakhs. Finally, we will never be able to control **Price Index** and to achieve **Economical Growth** in another 50 years. We should not make any delay to bring back all the foreign deposits of billionaires/ millionaires inclusive of all leaders to stabilize the Price Index and Economical Growth.

Laxmi Nayaran

**The Justice,**
**Supreme Court, High Courts & Tribunals**
**Corporate Consultants,**
**A. J. C. Bose Road, Kolkata-700017**

Sir,

## SUB: REVISED FIFTH EDITION OF MY BOOK - "EVOLUTION OF HUMAN BEINGS AND SOCIETY"

My above-mentioned Book, which is now further, revised incorporating few sample letters and one foreword of **Maa Mother Mahasweta Devi,** recipient of **Jnanpith and Raman megasayasay award,** which has been affixed with **PREFACE.**

SB is has to writen this letter to your honour enclosing herewith the above-mentioned two Books for controlling extortionate tendency to accumulate unaccounted source of money from people who are senior citizens and are living with piteous condition in the society. High profile dignitaries in national label retired are joining in senior citizens forum for catching poor senior citizens to accumulate unaccounted source of income.

SB is one of the victim who had registered his case against his brothers for not allowing him for construction in the undivided land with the above mentioned firm on ............. by paying Rs.......... after 10% discount of their normal charges being a life member of ......, ...... also a life member. And also on.......... he paid Rs........... for first counseling without ny result. When he has asked for the report of his attendant brothers' sayings, which should have been recorded in the separate counseling room, but SB came back without any report. He is living with his own savings of ......... approximately, per month and for all the various legal expenses he is managing from sanctioned O.D. from unutilized balances with various banks. With the interest presently, he is in debt of about Rs........ Since additional two percentage of interest has become unbearable he did close the O.D. A/c with Axis Bank, Golpark, liquidating my fixed deposit with the bank. One day SB requested to IARP's,. Vice President, Sri .......... for little help to request Justice Sri............. for solution of pending case in Alipore Police Court so that he can arrange one permanent office in his constructed building for senior citizens. After more than one month on his return from abroad SB got an appointment to meet him. Finally your honour has transferred my case to Sri...... firm's panel senior advocate,..........., Behala, Kolkata directing me to carry cash of Rs............ for appearing on hearing date of ........... but since it is state case his appearing will not be allowed and ultimately my two cases are again registered with Sri......... on......... by paying Rs........ his second case for Sri......, Sole proprietor of M/s ............, who had cheated SB with total amount of Rs......... approximately. After number of visits having number of petitions draft, SB could get one final draft petition on dated.......... to be filed in Chandan Nagar, copy attached, and the said draft if submit to the Court whose fate will be as his existing case which is running 5 years without even charge hearing. Ultimately SB could file this cheating case through some other Advocate in Alipore jurisdiction to additional Judicial Magistrate Court by paying only Rs........ on........., and FIR has also been lodged in Kolkata Police

Station during .......... SB would like to mention one incident happened in the office of Sri ............., where one M.A. LLB, Advocate ......... earlier working in a private company could not continue in the job later on obtained advocate practice license managing practice consulting senior advocate for preparing final petition.

Unfortunately, he was of SB's elder brother's advocate and later on advocating for him. On his advice, SB decided to file a suit against his brother and paid him Rs...... as advance, purchased one new Mobile for his wife's name, given his P.C. for his learning and every day SB used to come to teach him computer. The said advocate gave him dictation for preparing petition but on receipt of threatening call from his elder brother that he is a political leader and can spoil any body's life. Then he did not submit the petition. He never put his present on hearing day of any case, which he manages by some other advocate. One day SB saw him sitting in the office for Mr. .............................. immediately SB took permission from Mr. .............. and left the office. Some other day when Mr. ............. came back from Hospital after operation SB met him and showed him his petition to Honourable Bar Council against Sri ....... for refund of excess of Rs........... submitted on............... However, there also, he applied his influence and SB's petition never placed on Board until date. This person started sabotaging his case by giving all wrong information of SB's family matters to the opponent party's advocate for submitting an application to the Court to include in SB's Case File making his character assassination under section 239. Copy of this application and SB's complaint to Honourable Bar Council against Sri.........

shown to…….. Sr……. and when SB requested for some help to take action against said advocate, Sri………… told "he is my advocate cast" and he cannot help to take any action. And next after few days he told that "generally for filling petition I take rupees ten to fifteen thousand and for hearing I take rupees five thousand". Sri……… also a senior citizen like me but difference he is sick of accumulating money at this old age where I am unfit to be entered in that office any more. Now SB requested your honour to be kind enough to arrange punishment to the accused advocate, Sri………… and help to get refund of his money through Honourable Bar Council. While passing through one Police Station undersigned has noticed, one judgment beautifully framed on the wall of that police station that your honour being Supreme Court Judge has established Human Right Act for West Bengal. When SB wanted to submit his complaint against above- mentioned cheater for FIR, S.I. told that he cannot force any criminal/ cheater and cannot take any action under Human Right Act without court order. But that cheater has told me that his associated parties are paying Rs…………. every month. SB is filling unsecured life in this present state of affairs developed after independence in this state.

Yours truly,

Laxmi Nayaran

**Hon'bl Chief Justice of India,**
**Supreme Court of India,**
**Tilak Marg, New Delhi - 110001**

**Respected Sir,**

**SUB: SIXTH EDITION OF MY BOOK -**
**"EVOLUTION OF HUMAN BEINGS AND SOCIETY"**

The Captioned Books are further revised incorporating few more sample letters, mentioned below, to Hon'bl Prime Minister of India,

Chairperson of West Bengal Human Rights Commission, Chief Justice of India and other various judges for clarifying the present political scenario including one foreword of **Mother, Mahasweta Devi,** recipient of **Jnanpith and Raman megsaysay award,** which has been affixed with **PREFACE.**

Sir! As per knowledge and observation of **'SB' (Sukumar Banerjee),** speaker of the Captioned Book, which clarified that British Ruler, had handed over the dynasty of our country to their Pets dividing into two Parts as India and Pakistan. Very cunningly, the British Ruler had handed over the reign of our country, India to one of their pet Indian family members. But well before at the time of discussion and negotiation **Father of the undivided nation, Bapu Mahatma Gandhi** objected saying that the **Netaji Subhash Chandra Bose** is the first national leader who should take over the reign of this country.

While handing over the reign of this country to their pet Indian family member the British ruler advised not to change the British law and divide and rule policy keeping alive all the religious fundamentalism, castism, tribal backward class etc. to keep the dynasty under own and/or successors' control forever. Likewise fourth generation of that British Indian family member is ruling the country. As per **"SB'S"** learning from B**iography- "India Wins Freedom" of Moulana Abdul Kalam Azad** written in Urdu and translated in English by **Humayun Kabir, Writer, Educationist, Phylosopher and Politician.** As per people's look out while reading the Biography one script especially on the British Indian family member did not include in the Biography, which is very much mysterious. As per people's knowledge during publication period the said British Indian, family member has destroyed that particular Script when he came to know about the script, which had been written especially for him.

Now presently the next Supreme King of our country has determined to accomplish his commitment to the World King without thinking of miseries of **80% (APL & BPL)** categories of **people of** the second largest populated country. To accomplish his commitment he is now planning to make another type of King from Judiciary Section so that he can crash any obstruction from any corner of the country to make his democratic dictatorship with all success. Now I would like to draw your kind attention to the West Bengal Judiciary anarchism, which is in detailed given in the captioned Book in Judicial Chapter. All advocates and all staffs will take cash in advance without any receipt if asked for receipt they will say advocates here never give any receipt. Next if general people ask for judicial stamp/stamps paper in any denomination vender will say not available and if we are prepared to give extra charge vender will take almost double and even if we go to any advocate from their advocate quota they will also charge one and half time or double. Next, any criminal case State vs respondent PP will submit his/her written statement in favour of Respondent on receipt of huge cash from the respondent then will take transfer to some other Department. And that written statement judge will keep pending without passing any order and without giving any next hearing date. All general 80% people are tortured like no bodies business. I am also one of the victims even after fulfilling all advocates' extortionate charges. Financial expertise of the present Supreme King by implementing globalization and liaise-fare system with unlimited democracy made all people crazy to become millionaire/billionaire by all unfair means and by which entire bureaucratic systems have become corrupt through 99% self centered power crazy political leaders. Now I am enclosing herewith the copies of following letters for your kind perusal for amending all British Act for the benefit of 80% people.

My humble pray to you to be kind enough to give justice to the 80% (BPL & APL) Categories of People and to take severe action against the anarchism of West Bengal Judiciaries/ Advocates Section and required amendment of all British Acts including West Bengal Human Rights Act. As per SB's feeling we are still Citizens of British Colony ruled by Self Centered Power Crazy corrupted Group of Leaders nominated by World Kings.

Thanking you,

**Honourable President of India,**
**Office of the President of India,**
**Raisinha Hill,**
**New Delhi - 110001**

Respected Sir,

## SUB: MY SIXTH EDITION BOOK -
## "EVOLUTION OF HUMAN BEINGS AND SOCIETY"

First, I express my sincere congratulation to you on your success of becoming Head of the Country. I may draw your kind attention of my earlier letter dated………. enclosing therewith my 4th Edition of the captioned Book that stated "Any leader's loyalty to the Royal Party who was the most trusted representative of the British Ruler who handed over the reign of this country to them, can hold a strong position in the country. As per **SB's** observation when you went to America to meet the Prime Minister of India for showing some white paper of some various scams linked with your predecessor as Finance Minister, which published in Times of India and finally UPA-II decided to upgrade your position to the highest post of the country. It is known to everybody that any lawyer/barrister from London is to be absorbed in the Government as per British Law and/or if nominated by World Kings. Your Highness! May I request your kind and sympathetic consideration for the 80% (APL & BPL) categories of people living in piteous condition in the country especially in West Bengal due to anarchism in the earlier Government ruled by self-centered power crazy leaders. I would also request you to read the captioned Book and one foreword of **Mother, Mahasweta Devi recipient of Jnanpith and Raman Megasayday Award** including some sample letters in Part-III Part-II and Part-I.

**The Chairperson**
**West Bengal Human Rights Commission,**
**Bhabani Bhavan, Alipore,**
**Kolkata - 700027**

Sir,

## SUB: REVISED FIFTH EDITION OF MY BOOK - "EVOLUTION OF HUMAN BEINGS AND SOCIETY" AND WEST BENGAL HUMAN RIGHT ACT

SB is a senior citizen of nearing to …. years living alone in one single room of his parental house coming back after 40 years from exile for keeping his service alive on transfer out of Bengal in the year ……. when a political party capture the reign of this state for destroying the industries and business atmosphere of this state. Coming back in the year ……. permanently to settle down in his parental house especially for his younger brother who was living with wife and two children in a calamitous condition and for another main object to register their father's occupied ………….. of land for making **Bridhyashram** for senior citizens for which he has registered one **NGO-………** …" mentioned above. After landing in Kolkata first, SB was encircled by various cheaters introduced as social activists, his own brothers, small business people who did induce him for getting monetary benefits after investing his last balance of small savings. Finally he is totally broken through various types of advocates supported by **Retired Justice Sri……….** **who established West Bengal Human Right Act and**

**presently as President of...................** wherein SB was also one of the life members.

SB's above mentioned history is replica of the 2$^{nd}$ Part of the captioned Book- **"EVOLUTION OF HUMAN BEINGS AND SOCIETY"** in which one foreword of **Mother Mahasweta Devi**, recipient of **Jnanpith and Raman Magsaysay award** has been affixed with **PREFACE** of the Book.

Now SB is giving below the case wise details of his sufferings and tortures by the hands of judiciary and civil protector, Police Force for extortionate demand from both the parties (Victims and Accused).

1.  **Case No...... by Complainant:.......... Vs.............. for criminal offence u/s 406&420**

A) For the above case first petition prepared by his elder brother's advocate, **Sri .............** who had received a threatening call from his elder brother................. and said advocate could not proceed further and SB had to file a petition No..... of dated ............ against that advocate to the Bar Council of West Bengal for getting refund of Rs........ Copy of the petition enclosed. But Bar Council could not place his petition to the Board of Chairman till date because he got an influence with senior advocates of the Bar Council. Some advocates are in the panel of **Justice............& Co**. SB did send a letter dated......... to Sri.......... and copy forwarded to the Bar Council on ............. Copies of the above petitions and letters enclosed herewith.

B) Finally the above mentioned case was prepared and submitted by Sri ............, Sr. Advocate to the Criminal Court of South 24 Parganas at Alipore on......... which is still hanging on charge hearing for which hearing date also not given and remain pending for passing the order since ........., last hearing date. Since this case is under PP, SB has taken the file from the said Advocate. And handed over to another Advocate, ......... for minimizing the high charges of fees. SB has prepared one Inducement Statement in support of documentary Statement submitted to the Judge on demand which PP did not accept and told that she will prepare as per Charge Sheet but I.O. of P.S.............…… station did not take so many valid documents which are included in the statement submitted to the Judge. This inducement statement all the above advocates did express unwilling to prepare including Justice .......... paneled advocates.

C) Above Captioned Book is laudable of **SB's** compassion for the silver haired senior citizens who will be turning into a fast growing **Apartheids** in the society. SB decided that the total ......... Cottahs of land for which SB spent more than Rs. ...... lakhs till now including interest of Rs......... approx per month on over draft from various banks @ 11.5% and 10.75% after keeping deposit of his securities with the banks for constructing **Bridhyashram** on 55% of promoters allocation after giving 45% to land owners including other neighbours' land. SB one NGO No............" **copy** enclosed.

2. **Second Case No........... 2007 submitted on.......
by.......... Vs Accused.......... u/s 200 to the South 24
Parganas Criminal Court at Alipore.**

The above Accused has taken money for the sum of
Rs............ on verbal contract of Rs...... for constructing
Boundary Wall of our ......... Cottahs of Plot. 5 years running
till date Police could not deliver Saman/Warrant

3. **Case No.................... Complainant-........._against
that person, C/o Smt............... Vs.................**

**A)** For this case first I came to ......... through our Vice
President of I.A.R.P........... and SB registered with **Justice
.........  & Co.** for the first case by paying Rs......... on 10%
discount being life member of.......... But **Justice ............**
did not take this case instead he handed over this case to his
paneled **Sri.......... Advocate, Sri ...........** on .......... and
specifically advised SB by **Justice...........** to carry Cash of
Rs......... instead of cheque to attend the charge hearing date
0n......... of SB's first case of BGR-......... mentioned above
in Sl. No.1 and for this 3$^{rd}$ case. After studying both the file he
stated first case is State Vs SB's brothers and PP has to attend
in favour of Complainant and for Sl. No. 3 Case file he has
kept the file and demanded for cheque of Rs....... on ..........
After few months **Sri ..........** did give SB his final draft
on....... for submitting to ..... on ......... which was wrong
and other advocate from.......... Court did advise to go to **or
to ............** where one good Advocate advised SB to submit
to Alipore, Kolkata. Then again SB went to **Advocate,** who
directed him to his friend, **Advocate.........** Who prepared the

petition and submitted on .......... to the Ld......... C. J. M. Alipure. Next after receiving Court Order, ....... P. S. did send SB Saman to report to I.O. Sri ......... on ......... and received a copy of FIR. On......... reported to I.O., Sri ......... with original documents and witness to sign the seizer list copy of which has been received latter after various communications. Thereafter on ......... and 0n ......... SB sent a letter to the Joint Commissioner (Crime......... with a request to call for all the documents as mentioned in the letter and to take the Accused under their custody. When SB could not find any response then he sent a letter dated ......... to the Deputy Commissioner of Police, South Subarban Div. (Jadavpur Div.)..,..... D.P. S. Road. Kolkata. Again 0n ............ I did meet the D.C. personally and D.C. over telephone had directed O. C.,......... P. S. to arrest the Accused and to produce the Arrest Order for his signature and SB had been advised to follow up O. C. ............. Copies of the above-mentioned letters and a copy of Court Order are enclosed herewith. Till date SB followed up with the I.O..,............. of, .......... P. S. to get the Accused under their control. They are so busy for disposing the daily direct FIR cases where they need not fulfill the requirement under W.B.H.R. Act., which require for Court Order cases. Direct FIR Cases can meet both ends for Complainant and for Accused. Investigation, recording etc. are not required if advocates are ready with all legal formalities for every individual case. These criminal advocates are making huse money sharing with Police Officer from both the parties, i.e. Complainant and Accused after bringing back the Accused from Court lock up within a day or two. Civil nature case also after wrapping criminal offence cover through General

Diary both, Advocates and Police Officers are packed up for solving/settling the disputes with mouth full honey. This subject Human Right Act facilitates the Police Station not to arrest any criminal accused without proper investigation with valid documents but to take honey from the Accused for giving him temporary relief daily basis or monthly basis. This statement is based on SB's third case's accused Cheater, Sri .......... has told that his Marwari Business Partners pay every month in cash to........... Police station for the above mentioned Case. And the said Police Station has framed the judgment of the **Judge** ............ on the front entry wall of the ............ **Police station.** Now I am giving below the status of my **Advocate, Sri ...............**

SB was introduced with this Advocate during the year 2008 and he used to call SB as uncle as he got married with his friend's daughter living in our Block. Friend's name is Sri .............. which is also a communication address of the Advocate. When become very close, he used to show SB his day to day business transactions maintained in a big diary and total income during the year up to............. was Rs......... approximately. He used to keep one Branded....... Car inside the .......... Police Station for personal use by Officer-In-Charge and almost every day he used bring one criminal case for arrest and to release the same accused on lump sum settlement. Since he was not so conversant with writing a petition he used to keep one partner from his paneled advocates. For all of SB's cases he will ask to write SB's own case petition. There was one very big transaction with............. which has been caught by I. T. Enforcement cops and got cleared by his Chartered Accountant. With SB also made a verbal contract to settle our brothers Case mentioned above for Rs......... and given Rs......... advance but could not do and refunded the same step by step. Lastly SB paid Rs.......... bearer cheque from O.D. Account with SBI ............ Branch which he sent through his assistant, Sri.......... for withdrawing money waiting in queue. Then SB came to bank for his own work, took the cheque back, taken cash through ATM Debit Card and given to that Assistant. This money he demanded for advance for arresting the Accused, Sri ............ of for 3$^{rd}$ Case mentioned above. He could not do because his entry has been restricted in the.......... Police Station and his Branded Car also withdrawn from the Police station when complete overhauling done in the ........ Police Station by the Present **C.M.** including all other Police stations in Kolkata. Sir! If immediate I.T. Enforcement raid is taken up for seizing all his manual written Diaries his yearly Income can be worked out not less than Rs.......... Lakhs. He has already completed one 3 Story Building in ............., in Poss. local area. Now he is changing his business in Real Estate Business Field.

As per observation/opinion of **'SB'**, speaker of this 'Book' in 6$^{th}$ edition regarding Justice ............ who had established this WBHR Act for the benefit of Business Communities who are the financial ruler of our State's economy. Sri.......... has got two Office Premises and also one residential flat in ........... Next he could manage another residential Block where he is now residing. This WBHR Act established for all Cheaters, Business Communities, Black marketers etc. and not for general people. If C.B.I enquiry could be arranged for Justice.......... the above opinion about WBHR Act will be cleared.

Now SB prays that your honour would be gracious to give justice for SB's above mentioned three cases including his Case No.36 to Bar Council mentioned above U/s Advocate Act, 1961 against another Advocate.

**Now Karma Yogi, SB who is living alone deserted by all his relatives is moving in courts finding no alternative and thinking how to start 'Bridhyashram' for rendering Seva to helpless senior citizens who are fast growing condemned 'APARTHEIDS' in the society. God may shower His blessings on SB, so that he may continue in his struggle against injustice meted out to him in various quarters and go ahead with plan of setting up an Old-age Home for the condemned 'APARTHEIDS' who crossed golden age."**

# INDIAN DEMOCRACY

The British Ruler did hand over the reign of our country, India, to one of their pet Indian family members in democratic Platform advising to rule the country as per established law and Divide & Rule policy keeping alive all casteism, religious fundamentalism etc. Therefore, the generation to generation his predecessors can rule the country. Accordingly, numbers of Rulers/Kings have increased from Single to Thousands to Lakhs in three Categories, as **Administrative, Financial and Judiciary**. They have made **Burgeon ruling Platform of 20% Burgeon people namely:-1. All Political Leaders, 2. All Bureaucrats, 3. All Professionals, 4. All Industrialists, 5. All Business Communities are ruling over 80% APL & BPL(APL- "above poverty level" & BPL- "below poverty level)** categories of people in the Federal System of Democratic Country. Our Society is paternal system of Society since beginning when Society formed.

**There was a message, from educationist and great orator, Bipin Chandra Pal, which is published by the Editor of 'Statesman' on 22 May 1932 that "Democracies are notoriously ungrateful. They use man to the utmost limit for their physical and mental power and discard them and throw them on the scrapheap".**

This message is true to the knowledge of every politically educated person who understood that the present so-called democracies have become weapons for some group of **KING-PARTIES** as dictator to rule this democratic country in the shape of Anarchism and Nepotism with autocracy.

In any country Human Beings are the main Assets in the Country. We should utitlise them 100% for the country's development. 100% utilisation will create invention/discovery from the Universe. Whereas our Political Leaders/Kings are looking after their own Cadres/Workers only to keep their Power intake.

Indian Democracy can not remove corruption by any means because the entire Nation/Country ruled by **Political Leaders of Assembly and of Parliament as per direction of 20% Burgeon People mentioned above.**

Foreign Deposits more/or less 20 Billion Dollars deposited by some of Political Leaders and others from **20% Burgeon People,** which cannot be withdrawn and/or cannot display their individual names. This money will be utilised in hard Cash by Howalla transactions for Election Purpose. All Political Parties require cash money for paying their cadres, leaders and for propaganda/publicity to keep the Power intake. Hence they have to go to **20% Burgeon People.**

Government's strong efforts for the overall development for the Country inviting other developed countries' help and foreign Depositors' investments. But maximum benefits enjoyed by **20% Burgeon People.** They all are mostly making Cash transactions, especially all Political Leaders, all Bureaucrats, all Professionals and all Business Communities. And they get all helps from Government Organisations/Institutions by receiving Cash in exchange of transfering benefits. Various incidences are highlighted in the form of Sample Letters in Author's Main Book - **"Evolution of Human Beings and Society"** Especially in the State of West Bengal under **Kolkata Municipal Corporation Act** established in **1876 by British Ruler** Independent Parallel Government controlled by total Bureaucrats where only few Elected Political Leaders whose advices are not binding only eye witness personally benefitted and some percentage given to the Government in Cash which utilised for Cadres/Workers Salary and party's publicity. And again Government will add in the Government's Expenditures on A/c of donation to all Clubs, Muscle Power in all Blocks for Political Parties. Such a Huge Establishment could not make any infrastructures in any Blocks for all maintenance works which are done by contractors must be on 40/60 ratio with government in cash. Author's Main Book Speaker **'SB'** has given technical **Know-How** for making **Kolkata** as **London** having similiar Geographical background of **London.** also the same **Technical Know-How** mentioned in this Book. **'SB'** also sugested in sample letters to Chief Justice of India

to abolish the **KMC Act** so that more or less one lac youth can get a permanent Job to build up the Infrastructures and do the smooth maintenance works through elected Block Councilors.

Presently here all labours/technicians do not accept Peace Rate but insist for Contract Rate on Business policy.

In Hinduism, there are four **Yugas** such as **Satya, Treta, Drapad**, and **Cali Yuga** presently running. **Man-Pita (Father)** is the head of the family. Man is dominating in the family as well as in the Society. Women populations are increasing and they are capable of managing the entire Society in much better than men if they are not **Self Centered Power Crazy women**. Factually, Woman is much more superior to Male Person. First, Woman is the creator of Human Beings. Man deposits seeds and Woman preserves the seeds feed them and bring them in the Society. Woman is much sexier than Male Person, but Woman has controlling element i.e. **Diffidence/(Lajja)/Shyness** which controls the sex of Woman. Sex is natural requirement and demand. As per **Unani and Ayurvedic's** explanation woman body's has eight places filling of Sex sensation. However, man has got only in two places. In the '**Quran**', Dress Code for Woman specified for complete body **cover** with **Veil (Borkha)**. Now the modern Society's Woman prefers to expose their body for beautification, competition in Fashion Parade and elsewhere.

Author's main **Book-'Evolution of Human Beings and Society'** given detailed analysis for **Self-Government** systems from Block level to District Level.

To implement the said systems Government has to pass Bill for taking control of all Clubs, Temples, Mosques, Churches and other religious Centers under Government control and to set up one **BDO Office** for administering the **Block** for developing the followings:-

All unemployed people as per Mobile Employment Exchange Record in the Block should get job. In all religious Centers, all devotees should come as usual to pray almighty as per individual's religious belief in their respective temples, mosques, Churches and any other respective Centers after depositing their contributions, any articles etc to the **Block Office**. Block Offices employed attendants attached to temples, Mosques, Churches and other religious Centers will accompany them to the Worship Place. All Priests, Pandas, Imams, Moulabis, Fathers and other Religious Heads will get remuneration every month from the Devotees' contributions and other valuables from the **Block Office**. All unemployed **Club** members will get job as Security Man or as per their Skilled/Unskilled capability. Total Income from **Club** activities will be under control of **BDO Office**. Self-Employed Individuals in any business and/or any Professions should register their working details in **BDO Office** to contribute certain percentage from their Income for Block Developments such as 100% Education, Health, Cultural activities etc. No Cadres of any Political Parties are required to visit to any Business and Professionals' Offices to collect the Funds for their Political Parties' requirements for paying salary to their cadres only and maintaining all expenses for parties' propaganda, vague slogan etc. instead all unemployed will get their respective jobs in their Block through BDO Office. Political Parties funds requirements are the main cause of corruptions in entire Bureaucratic systems. All political Parties' leaders have interlinked relations in the corruption. They abuse stating '**Dishonest**' to each other but cannot go further for fear of getting gluey mud in their character. There is no ambiguity that most of the leaders are suffering from **Revenue Cancer** and no chance of getting cure because their Million/ Brillion Dollars in foreign Banks will remain unclaimed. What a pity and shameful matter for us. Now to cure all the **Revenue Cancer patients** we have to establish **MAA, MATI & MANUSH Society.** First think for **MAA-(Bharat MAA)** for whom we have to change the political structure i.e. Federal

Systems to Presidential Systems elected by the people, of the people and for the people. Next to choose Leader for President, who thinks for people from **'MATI', (Block to District label).** Next to choose 'MANUSH' (Man or Woman) and for this we have to go to Hinduism Story of **Treta Yuga**, when **Ram** worshiped for arrival of **'MAA' "Durg**a" to kill '**Ravana'**. We can choose from only Woman, who is superior to Man, but does not possess any Self-Centered Power Crazy Mentality except developing Ego and direct Injection to all **Revenue Cancer Patients** to establish" **MAA, MATI & MANUSH Society".** Any Leader from any State if claim that he is only eligible for becoming competent Head of the Country by showing his only Industrial growth which benefitted only **20% Burgeon People** of total population not for **80% of APL & BPL** categories of people. **SB,** Speaker of the main Book questioned that by Industrial growth can any body prove 100% employment, 100% Education, 100% Health and 100% secured life?

Now **'SB'** is going to analyse religious fundamentalism and some idea to remove inhuman treatment by Fundamentalist through his **Self-Government System** already explained in the foregoing method in the **Author's Main Book mentioned above**.

## 1. Fundamentalism in Hinduism:

In Hinduism, there were 33 Crores Spiritual Persons as Gods and Goddesses arrived to remove inhuman treatment by Fundamentalist to establish peace and humanity in the Society. Out of them, there are Supreme Spiritual Persons-Gods arrived in four different **Yuga (Period)** like **Sri Bishnu/Brahma in Satya Yuga, Sri Ram in Treta Yuga, Sri Krishna in Drapad Yuga and in Cali Yuga:-Sri Budhyadeb, Sri Jaganath, Sri Chaitanya Mahaprabhu, Sri Ramakrishna, Sri Pareshnath /Tirthankara, Sri Guru Nanak etc.**

Some **Spiritual Persons/Gods** created some powerful Gods and Goddesses through sexual activities. As an Example **Sri Shiva -God** who was the **King** of **Kailash Parbat** and throughout the years and years was on **Yoga/Sadhana** of **Soul**. And become so powerful strong **Person-God** that **He** could transfer his power to **Ravana** who was worshiping **Sri Shiva** later on made that **Sri Shiva** his captive and whenever, **Ravana** moving for conquer, he used to carry **Sri Shiva** on his shoulder. However, **Sri Shiva** told o **Ravana** that if he keeps **Sri Shiva** for any reason on the land he would not be able to pull him out from that place. **Ravana** was under tremendous urinal pressure and he has to keep him on **Deoghar Land, now in Jharkhand State**, is the **First Shiva Temple** in India. There is another story about the **Stone image of Sri Shiva.** 'MAA-Pārbati' wife of Sri Shiva, was daughter of **Janak**, Maharaja of Himalaya. 'MAA- Pārbati' was worshiping **Sri Shiva. O**ne day, when she was in the **Kailash Sarobar** with her friends for taking bath, **Sri Shiva** nearby was in inanimate condition in **Yoga/Sadhana** on one mountain. **Sri Shiva** suddenly got wake up when some women were taking bath with high volume sounding games. **Sri Shiva's** Sex excitement awakened his penis, which he extended long towards those women, and those who were looking to the long penis started loud utterance expressing joy but **MAA-Pārbati** inserted that Penis in her Bush. Latter on **MAA-Pārbati's** friend groups cut that Penis. The first **Image of Sri Shiva** in **Deoghar Temple** is in the shape of **Cut Penis** inserted in the Bush **of MAA-Pārbati.** Throughout the country on **Shiva Day,** people are worshiping this image sacredly so that they get same power like **Sri Shiva**. Now **SB's** queries why religious fundamentalists should kill **Mahatma Gandhi** who arrived in this country as **God** to establish Humanity with secularity without violence. And, why world famous painter, **M. F. Husain** has to leave his country for not doing any crime but for making his own thinkable Goddess's Image. It is wrong **Fatwa** when we can worship the Image of our **Shiva-God Image and/or Stone made Image**.

## 2. **Muslim's Islamic Religion in 'Quran' & Christian Religion in 'Bible'**

Both the religions are accepted by each very friendly. Moreover, both the Religions are merciful and they believe, God will punish them for their crime. Now in India also Religious harmony extended in marital relation with each other Love. Moreover, India is a Secular, Democratic Country. **God, Christ** direct from **Mother Marry,** sacrificed himself for the cause of peace and humanity. **Prophet, Hazarat Muhammad**, illiterate, cannot read and write anything but Angel, messenger of **Allah (Almighty)**, bestowed **Allah's Prophecy** through **Prophet's** versions in 'Quran'. In **Quran**, there is no direct punishment announced like **'Fatwa'** to any one for any crime but left on **Allah** who will decide. We should not encourage any Fundamentalists' Group to create terrorism in the Society creating inhuman crimes. **SB** feels all-religious Heads-Pundits',

Gurus, Imams, Moulabis, and Fathers; jointly conduct one Convention to instigate/inspire to all religious people to conduct prayer everyday to strengthen their brainpower and to gain the following benefits of **Health and Mind**:

1. Improved 'Immune Function'
2. Reduced risk of death from heart attack and stroke
3. Reduced stress and increased peace of mind
4. Reduction and Elimination of panic attacks, anxiety and depression
5. Reduced impacts from chronic pain
6. A more positive, happy out-look on 'Life'
7. A healthier, longer, more fulfilled 'Life'

In addition of above prayers we should invite them to attend Temples, Gurdwaras, Churches, Mosques and other any religious Places on various occasions announcing any auspicious Day celebration through broadcasting channels. For all these we should insist Government to take over all the Religious Places and set up one **BDO office** to manage the situation. By this, Income will increase and everybody will get good job so that idle brain will not choose any criminal jobs.

In view of the above **SB** feels that the **'Fatwa'** announced for **Writers**, **Taslima Nasrin & Salman Rushdie** can be withdrawn. **SB** feels that if Government passes the Bill for taking over all the Clubs, Religious Places can remove all Terrorists set-ups moving door to door from **Block label to District label** by giving them employment through Mobile Employment Exchange and Broad Casting Media Channel for over all development of **80% BPL and APL categories** of people then **'MAA. MATI & MANUSH' Society** is established.

Once the above Society is established then unlimited democratic rights of **20% Burgeon peoples** can be synchronized for stopping their Nepotism and anarchism in the Society over **80% BPL and APL Categories of people.**

As per Swami Vivekananda, Casteism originated from division of labours details of which are given in the **Autor's** Main **Book mentioned above:-**

**First:** the Tasks of **Saints/Father/Brahmins/Gurus/ Moulabis'** to impart gnayana (knowledge) to all and then became the Ruler of the Society in **Satya Yuga.**

**Second:** the Tasks of **Khatryas/Warriors** whose works are to protect the Country and all man beings from enemies and then became the Ruler of the Society in **Treta Yuga and Drapad Yuga.**

**Third:** the Tasks of **Baishya/Bania/Businessmen** who is providing all commodities and services to all human beings and then started controlling the entire economy and became the Ruler

**Fourth: Sudras/Workers** are the ones who perform all various works like cleanliness and other various activities/works for all human beings in the society. These **Sudras/Workers** are becoming poor and poorer; they may revolt for making **'Proletariat Dictatorship'** to rule the Society. **All these four divisions of labours are categorized as 'Caste'.**

Presently in the **Burgeon Ruling Platform,** your unlimited democratic rights for **20% Burgeon people** ruling over **80% APL & BPL Categories of people** cannot control **Price Index.** In the present **Burgeon Ruling Platform** 99% people are vitiated to earn extra money by cheating, coercion, false representation etc. Everybody wants to become business man. Now nobody wants to work on piece rate. All technicians want to work on contract basis. Latest **TOI'S** report one Electrician is earning more than one Engineer. Like was all Service men/Professionals are looting money by all means especially there are new business categories like Commission Agents, Media etc. who can overturn the Dynasty propagating false slogans, false statistical reports financed by **A Group of Companies**. In the **Author's Main Book mentioned above** suggested in the **Price Index Chapter** profit margin 3 to 4 times in **MRP Price** on factory rate should be reduced and fresh cultivated products in retail markets every handling, charging more than 100% to 200% profits should be reduced after addition of transportation charges only.

In the Shopping Mall, retail-prices are more than in the open retail market price. Moreover, in Whole Sale Mall fresh cultivated products' rates are more than Open Retail Market.

**Author** strongly condemns Emergency Food Bill for poor people. This is another deception to the **80% BPL & APL** Categories of people. You are well aware that your **Fair Price Shop** is very much-corrupted unit in the Society. This is only for Government's own Party dominated States for election campaign and those people benefitted will earn extra money by selling in the market on high rate. In addition, your distribution bureaucratic system is dangerously corrupted unit in the

**Burgeon Ruling Platform.** We are Second Largest Populated Country in the World. You are trying to implement all systems of World Kings whose population is 1/3$^{rd}$ of our Population. Implementation of all Financial Expertise rewarded in the country of World King will boost up status of **20% Burgeon People** to increase corruption, terrorism etc. in the Country. Also suggested 100% employment by implementing Self Government Systems in Gram Panchayat and in the City. For this, we have to arrange **National Religious Convention** to support **Emergency Bill** for controlling all States' **Religious Associations/ Institutions** and all **Clubs' Sports and Cultural activities'** development under guideline of Central Government. For this, we have to establish **States' Sena** to visit door to door along with **BDO Officer** for preparing Bio-Data of every member of the house for their development.

3. <u>**Money Market/Share Market:**</u>

This Market is only for **20% Burgeon people's interest.** In addition, your full-hearted endeavours to boost up their interest you are after **FDI** Investment for higher **interest.** In addition, your full-hearted endeavours to boost up their interest you are after **FDI** Investment for higher percentage of **NAV** in Share Market for selling the shares on higher rate to make them Billionaire. By this system, **80% APL & BPL categories of people's** calamitous condition is deteriorating as per details given below:

Share Market under control of **SEBI** which is again under control of '**A' Group of companies'** leadership for manipulating under guideline of Reliance Group, Financial

King of our Country. This King is continuously satisfying The Government's Kings, all Bureaucrats, Ministers, etc. through all **'A' Group of companies** by giving their own shares at lowest price so that the same shares can be sold in Boom period. In exchange, they are dictating the Government to pass the Bill for extra ordinary power to **SEBI**. So that **SEBI** can interfere in all other non-member companies' business affairs registered under Companies Act with Incorporation Certificate from Ministry of Corporate Affairs including authority to collect money from public against deposit Certificate, Debenture Certificate and Redeemable Preference Share Certificate when **FDI** investment is not responding. If you remember during 1994 Chairman of **UTI** made a deal with Reliance Group to crash down the **US-64 M.F. Scheme** in exchange of receiving Reliance share @Rs.1/- for his own shares when we **all 80% of BPL & APL categories people** were getting **26% dividend** per annum. Finally, that scheme is now closed. Earlier Government has put huge unpaid outstanding **EPF** deposit in Share Market and possibly entire **EPF** deposit of all salaried personnel also will be invested in Share Market by opening an individual Bank A/c where dividend/profit will be credited to all Individual A/c. And Author's experience Brokers of all **'A' Group of companies** through their strong manipulation will crash down **NAV** rate and nothing will add in the Individual A/c for indefinite Bull period.

As per Author's opinion that EPF entire amount should be kept in Mutual Fund under Debt Scheme so that some amount will be credited in Individual Account. Next, this **SEBI** with its self-styled with undue power started sending notice to the various Registered Ltd. Company and incorporated with

Ministry of Corporate Affairs not to collect any deposit from Public and all collected amount to refund to Public. Due to this notice, Crores of 80% of BPL & APL Categories of people are suffering for non-receipt of their Principal and monthly return for long period. Immediately Government should take possession of all companies Assets/properties and announce for auction to get the money back to refund the investors' Deposit and employees of all those ceased companies. Alternative Government should take over all running establishments to pay off employees' salary and to clear Investors/Depositors dues at the earliest possible. If you have little humanitarian sympathy for **80% BPL and APL categories of people** please stop all **CBI** enqueries, **ED** raids and **SEBI**'s orders to close all hundreds of small Industries/Business Organisations due to which crores of people are suffering and you are filling your **20% Burgeon Peoples** pockets and your Bankers Income. Your absolute majority in the Government is establishing your dictatorship for the benefit of your 20% Burgeon People. You are well aware that your entire Bureaucratic systems and your Ministry level are corrupted like no bodies business as per daily News Paper Reports. Your earlier Finance Ministry as per last year's News Paper Report there was one white paper came out for **2G Scam** and other various Scams linked with your Finance Minister's name, which with craftiness method the matter got clean chit. This Ministry's I.T. Department under the table clearing all disputes every day. In my case I am Nil Return Holder forgot to claim my TDS refund but with the help of subordinate with I.T.O.'s approval, I got my refund as per Credit shows in the Book of my Pan No. Account as per normal procedure by giving cash 10% to 15%. Another Case of mine with one Advocate who was torturing me for huge undue cash receipt I have given one detailed letter to **C.I.T**. enforcement Department for the said Advocate whose yearly Income nearly to Rs. Fifty Lakh.

Sample letters of the Author's main **Book** mentioned above to earlier Government for Attn Prime Minister to pass the **Emergency Bill** for collecting Infrastructure Tax on Profit/Income quarterly from the following **Burgeon People** @ 5% on Rupees 5 lakhs to 10 lakhs, 10% on over 10 lakhs to 50 Lakhs, 15% on over 50 Lakhs to 10 Crores and 20% over 10 Crores and above.

1. **All Bureaucrats arrange ministers' Cash requirement**
2. **All Professionals maximum dealings in Cash**
3. **All Business communities maximum in Cash**
4. **All Industrialists**
5. **All Political Leaders called Revenue Cancer Patients**

Above collection will help **80% BPL & APL of categories of People** to get 100% employment, 100% Education, 100% the Health Care to maintain the internal peace and security in the whole nation from extortion, terrorism, separatism, communalism /fundamentalism, corruption etc. these also will make improvement of national feeling and disciplined culture by curing all **Revenue Cancer Patients** from **Burgeon People.** Author's humble appeal to the government to pass an amendment bill for the following Acts which are slow poisining for **80% APL & BPL** categories of people for not getting justice under most corrupted judicial systems details of which are given in author's main Book mentioned above.

1. **WEST BENGAL HUMAN RIGHTS ACT**

   a) Elaborete details are given in sample letter of Author's **Main Book** mentioned above.

   b) **Criminal Acts**: Convicted party is allowed to move free for unlimited years on his will and wish for not fulfilling the complainants' complaints and there is no financial relief for the injustice to the Complainant.

   c) **Civi Code Act**: This act also same status as above for indefinite detention for justice.

**BONDE MATARAM**

Printed in the United States
By Bookmasters